Developing Vocabulary
for College Thinking

Developing Vocabulary for College Thinking

Sherrie L. Nist
University of Georgia

Michele L. Simpson
University of Georgia

Allyn and Bacon

Boston ▪ London ▪ Toronto ▪ Sydney ▪ Tokyo ▪ Singapore

Vice President, Humanities: *Joseph Opiela*
Series Editorial Assistant: *Julie Hallett*
Marketing Manager: *Melanie Goulet*
Production Editor: *Christopher H. Rawlings*
Editorial-Production Service: *Omegatype Typography, Inc.*
Composition and Prepress Buyer: *Linda Cox*
Cover Design: *Kay Petronio*
Electronic Composition: *Omegatype Typography, Inc.*

Library of Congress Cataloging-in-Publication Data

Nist, Sherrie L. (Sherrie Lee)
    Developing vocabulary for college thinking / Sherrie L. Nist, Michele L. Simpson.
      p. cm.
    Includes index.
    ISBN 0-205-32326-X (alk. paper)
      1. Vocabulary—Problems, exercises, etc. 2. Critical thinking—Problems, exercises, etc. I. Simpson, Michele L. II. Title.
    PE1449 .N495 2001
    428.1—dc21

                                                      00-059419

Cover Photo: Copyright © PhotoDisc

Printed in the United States of America

10 9 8 7 6 5 4 3 2 1   05 04 03 02 01 00

CONTENTS

PREFACE

Developing Vocabulary for College Thinking is a structured approach to learning vocabulary that takes into consideration the importance of many different types of interactions with words. Based on current research and theory in the field of vocabulary, the text teaches new words embedded in the context of reading selections. In addition, we stress that there is no one clean and perfect way to learn vocabulary. It certainly isn't as simple as using either dictionary or context or word elements. Rather, *Developing Vocabulary* stresses using a combination of all three approaches, pulling in students' prior knowledge whenever possible and teaching a variety of generative vocabulary strategies that students will be able to apply on their own, beyond the course for which they are using this book. As developmental reading instructors for many years, we have used these materials and activities with our own students and have witnessed positive results. Not only have we watched students' knowledge of words grow, but students using the strategies and techniques described in *Developing Vocabulary* have also improved their reading comprehension and writing well beyond our classrooms.

The text is divided into two parts. Part I, which includes the first four chapters, sets the stage for further intense practice in Part II. Chapter 1, "Knowing a Word," focuses on what it means to know a word conceptually. It presents the different stages of word knowledge and discusses why it is important to develop an extensive vocabulary. Chapter 2, "Generative Vocabulary Strategies," discusses numerous strategies that students can use as they learn words in this text and beyond. Chapter 3, "Dictionary Use," takes an unconventional approach to teaching students how and when to use a dictionary. Although we have a section in this chapter about how to "read" dictionary entries, the major focus is on how to judge definitions appropriately and how a dictionary can be used in conjunction with other generative strategies. Chapter 3 also introduces word etymologies. Chapter 4, "Word Elements," discusses how to use prefixes, roots, and suffixes as another means of unlocking word meaning.

In each of those four chapters, students also have the opportunity to learn numerous new words taken from books, newspaper articles, and magazine articles. Each chapter contains three readings. The first selection is used to teach the strategies introduced in the chapter in conjunction with a section in each chapter called "Building Blocks." The remaining two readings provide further practice in using the strategies and introduce additional new words. Before each reading, students self-evaluate and then engage in Vocabulary Activities that lead them to understand words conceptually: Figuring It Out, Practicing It, and Applying It. Some selections also have Extending activities that provide additional practice.

At the end of each chapter is an Evaluating activity, in which students evaluate their word knowledge by taking a test that covers the words presented in all three selections.

The three chapters in Part II reinforce the strategies taught in Part I and provide intensive practice for students to learn words conceptually. In addition to reviewing some of the strategies introduced in Part I through a Building Blocks Revisited section, each chapter contains three reading selections with numerous words targeted for learning. As in Part I, the reading selections in Part II also have Figuring It Out, Practicing It, Applying It, Extending, and Evaluating activities.

A final comment about the text: Although *Developing Vocabulary* has vocabulary development as its goal, students also learn strategies that improve their overall comprehension. To this end, each reading also has a Comprehension Quick-Check Quiz, which is located in the Instructor's Guide, to help students assess how much they have understood. Such an approach encourages students to go beyond memorizing basic definitions to learning information in a more conceptual way. In addition, we also feel that discussion about words and concepts is important if students are to grow to their potentials. Therefore, throughout the text, we encourage instructors to talk about the readings and the words found in them. We also recommend that students do some of the activities with a study partner or in a small group.

As teachers ourselves, we have enjoyed this approach with our students and have found that our students have grown in their knowledge of words and have incorporated them into their writing and speaking. We hope that your experiences and the experiences of your students will be as positive as ours.

Acknowledgments

Numerous individuals who were either directly or indirectly involved with the completion and subsequent publication of this book deserve our thanks. The idea for writing *Developing Vocabulary for College Thinking* stemmed from the need we observed in our students. Hence, first and foremost, we owe a great deal of thanks and appreciation to them. During the past several years, they have validated our philosophical beliefs about teaching vocabulary, informed us emphatically about the kind of reading that interested them, and, perhaps most importantly, tried out a wide variety of activities important to our philosophical base. During this entire process, we have learned how to encourage long-term vocabulary growth. In a sense, this text is a culmination of what our students have taught us, as well as what we have taught them.

Second, our thanks to reviewers Kathy Beggs, Pikes Peak Community College; Judy Kupersmith, St. Petersburg Junior College; Linda C. Lisman, Binghamton University; Natalie Miller, Joliet Junior College; and Mark Szymanski, Lane Community College, for their suggestions for the development of this text. We believe that incorporating these reviewers' suggestions has strengthened *Developing Vocabulary for College Thinking* and made it useful for a large cross-section of college students.

Third, we thank our editor at Allyn and Bacon, Joe Opiela, for his help. In addition, our thanks to Katherine Coyle and others at Omegatype Typography for their careful scrutiny of this manuscript and their helpful suggestions.

Last, and certainly not least, we would like to thank our respective families for their support during our work on this book. So, to our biggest fans—Steve, Kama, Mom, Dad, and Tom: we appreciate your love, patience, and support.

S.L.N.
M.L.S.

Developing Vocabulary
for College Thinking

PART I

Generative Strategies and Practice

The chapters in Part I give you tools to help you learn new words on your own and learn words well enough to incorporate them into your own writing and speaking. Chapter 1 addresses the importance of a large vocabulary and what it means to truly know a word. Chapter 2 focuses on a variety of strategies that you can use to learn words for future situations. Chapter 3 takes a unique look at using a dictionary, including word origins, or etymologies. Chapter 4 targets word elements—prefixes, roots, and suffixes.

Although the main purpose of the chapters in Part I is to give you the strategies you need to develop a life-long program of vocabulary learning, we also introduce many new words. Each chapter contains three selections—Readings A, B, and C—which are the sources of the targeted vocabulary words that you will be studying and learning. The readings provide a context in which to learn the words. Words from these selections are used to demonstrate and reinforce the vocabulary strategies taught in the Building Blocks section of each chapter.

Each reading is formatted in the following way:

Self-Evaluation—Before you read a selection, you will evaluate your current level of understanding of each targeted word from the selection.

Reading (A, B, and C)—Each chapter contains three selections. It is important to read each one so that you can see how the targeted (boldfaced) words are used in context.

Comprehension Quick-Check—After you read each selection, you will need to ask your instructor for a copy of the Comprehension Quick-Check Quiz. This step is important so that you can be sure you understood what you read.

1

Building Blocks—In the Building Blocks section of each chapter you will learn strategies to increase your vocabulary knowledge.

Figuring It Out—These activities will help you clarify the meanings of the targeted words. You should do these activities *after* you use the dictionary and any other strategies to help you determine possible definitions.

Practicing It—These activities give you useful practice with the targeted words.

Applying It—These activities help you learn the targeted words well enough that you will be able to use them in your own writing and speaking. These activities also help you remember the words on a long-term basis and at a conceptual level.

Extending (only with Reading C)—These activities help you stretch your vocabulary knowledge. The words in the Extending activities are drawn from Readings A, B, and C.

Evaluating—After reviewing and testing your understanding of the targeted words in a chapter, you will take an exam, which will test your mastery of all the words. The evaluation activities have various formats, similar to the ones you encounter in the Practicing It and Applying It sections. You will need to ask your instructor for these exams.

We encourage you to read the first four chapters carefully. We also encourage you not only to do the Vocabulary Activities but also to discuss the targeted words in class and to try to use them in your daily conversations and in your writing. Making a concerted effort to understand and try out the strategies presented in Part I will enable you to progress efficiently and effectively through the chapters in Part II. More important, Part I will give you tools to increase your vocabulary throughout your academic and personal life.

1 Knowing a Word

DID YOU KNOW?

The word *boycott* originated from Captain Charles Boycott, a landlord who treated his tenants unfairly. To get even, the tenants refused to work and intercepted his food and mail. Today if you *boycott* a company, you refuse to buy from that company.

Do you remember any of your past experiences with vocabulary improvement? If you are like most students, you were probably given 20 words a week that you had to look up in a dictionary so you could write a definition and sentence for each. Do you remember cramming madly for those Friday quizzes? Do you also remember immediately forgetting all those words the moment you escaped the classroom? If so, you are not alone. Those experiences in "expanding" your vocabulary may not have been effective or pleasant.

This textbook approaches vocabulary expansion differently, so you will be able to remember the new words you learn for your personal use. Before we discuss strategies that can increase vocabulary, however, we need to outline some basic notions that underlie the text. Hence, the purpose of this chapter is to explain why vocabulary learning is important and what it means to know a word "conceptually."

READING A

In each chapter there are three selections for you to read. The selections are taken from magazines and newspapers, as well as popular fiction and nonfiction books. "My Alma Mater," Reading A in Chapter 1, is an excerpt from

Malcolm X's autobiography. Perhaps you saw the movie based on Malcolm X's book. In this selection Malcolm X describes how he educated himself while in prison. We are sure you will find his methods interesting. Before reading the article and completing the Vocabulary Activities, evaluate your present understanding of each of the 12 targeted words. Circle 1, 2, or 3 to indicate how familiar you are with each word. Use the following guidelines to rate your understanding:

1 — I do not know this word at all. I have never before seen or heard this word.
2 — I recognize this word, but I do not know exactly what it means (partial understanding). I might be able to give some characteristics of the word, but I could not provide an exact meaning nor could I use the word in a sentence.
3 — I know this word because I can define it accurately and precisely (conceptual understanding). I know and understand what the word means when I see or hear it, and I can use it in a sentence.

Level of Understanding

atheism	1	2	3
dormant	1	2	3
emulate	1	2	3
engrossing	1	2	3
expounded	1	2	3
feigned	1	2	3
inevitable	1	2	3
quota	1	2	3
rehabilitation	1	2	3
riffling	1	2	3
riveted	1	2	3
vistas	1	2	3

My Alma Mater
by Malcolm X

The first man I met in prison who made any positive impression on me whatever was a fellow inmate, "Bimbi." I met him in 1947, at Charlestown. He was a light, kind of red-complexioned Negro, as I was; about my height, and he had freckles. Bimbi, an old-time burglar, had been in many prisons. In the license plate shop where our gang worked, he operated the machine that stamped out the numbers. I was along the conveyor belt where the numbers were painted.

Bimbi was the first Negro convict I'd known who didn't respond to "What'cha know, Daddy?" Often, after we had done our day's license plate **quota,** we would sit around, perhaps fifteen of us, and listen to Bimbi. Normally, white prisoners wouldn't think of listening to Negro prisoners' opinions on anything, but guards, even, would wander over close to hear Bimbi on any subject.

He would have a cluster of people **riveted,** often on odd subjects you never would think of. He would prove to us, dipping into the science of human behavior, that the only difference between us and outside people was that we had been caught. He liked to talk about historical events and figures. When he talked about the history of Concord, where I was to be transferred later, you would have thought he was hired by the Chamber of Commerce, and I wasn't the first inmate who had never heard of Thoreau until Bimbi **expounded** upon him. Bimbi was known as the library's best customer. What fascinated me with him most of all was that he was the first man I had ever seen command total respect . . . with his words.

Bimbi seldom said much to me; he was gruff to individuals, but I sensed he liked me. What made me seek his friendship was when I heard him discuss religion. I considered myself beyond **atheism**—I was Satan. But Bimbi put the atheist philosophy in a framework, so to speak. That ended my vicious cursing attacks. My approach sounded so weak alongside his, and he never used a foul word.

Out of the blue one day, Bimbi told me flatly, as was his way, that I had some brains, if I'd use them. I had wanted his friendship, not that kind of advice. I might have cursed another convict, but nobody cursed Bimbi. He told me I should take advantage of the prison correspondence courses and the library.

When I had finished the eighth grade back in Mason, Michigan, that was the last time I'd thought of studying anything that didn't have some hustle purpose. And the streets had erased everything I'd ever learned in school; I didn't know a verb from a house. . . .

Many who today hear me somewhere in person, or on television, or those who read something I've said, will think I went to school far beyond the eighth grade. This impression is due entirely to my prison studies.

It had really begun back in the Charlestown Prison, when Bimbi first made me feel envy of his stock of knowledge. Bimbi had always taken charge of any conversation he was in, and I had tried to **emulate** him. But every book I picked up had few sentences which didn't contain anywhere from one to nearly all of the words that might as well have been in Chinese. When I just skipped those words, of course, I really ended up with little idea of what the book said. So I had come to the Norfolk Prison Colony still going through only book-reading motions. Pretty soon, I would have quit even these motions, unless I had received the motivation that I did.

I saw that the best thing I could do was get hold of a dictionary—to study, to learn some words. I was lucky enough to reason also that I should try to improve my penmanship. It was sad. I couldn't even write in a straight line. It was both ideas together that moved me to request a dictionary along with some tablets and pencils from the Norfolk Prison Colony school.

I spent two days just **riffling** uncertainly through the dictionary's pages. I'd never realized so many words existed! I didn't know which words I needed to learn. Finally, to start some kind of action, I began copying.

In my slow, painstaking, ragged handwriting, I copied into my tablet everything printed on that first page, down to the punctuation marks.

I believe it took me a day. Then, aloud, I read back, to myself, everything I'd written on the tablet. Over and over, aloud, to myself, I read my own handwriting.

I woke up the next morning, thinking about those words—immensely proud to realize that not only had I written so much at one time, but I'd written words that I never knew were in the world. Moreover, with a little effort, I also could remember what many of these words meant. I reviewed the words whose meanings I didn't remember. Funny thing, from the dictionary first page right now, that "aardvark" springs to my mind. The dictionary had a picture of it, a long-tailed, long-eared, burrowing African mammal, which lives off termites caught by sticking out its tongue as an anteater does for ants.

I was so fascinated that I went on—I copied the dictionary's next page. And the same experience came when I studied that. With every succeeding page, I also learned of people and places and events from history. Actually the dictionary is like a miniature encyclopedia. Finally the dictionary's A section had filled a whole tablet—and I went on into the B's. That was the way I started copying what eventually became the entire dictionary. It went a lot faster after so much practice helped me to pick up handwriting speed. Between what I wrote in my tablet, and writing letters, during the rest of my time in prison I would guess I wrote a million words.

I suppose it was **inevitable** that as my word-base broadened, I could for the first time pick up a book and read and now begin to understand what the book was saying. Anyone who has read a great deal can imagine the new world that opened. Let me tell you something; from then until I left that prison, in every free moment I had, if I was not reading in the library, I was reading on my bunk. You couldn't have gotten me out of books with a wedge. Between Mr. Muhammad's teachings, my correspondence, my visitors—usually Ella and Reginald—and my reading of books, months passed without my even thinking about being imprisoned. In fact, up to then, I never had been so truly free in my life. . . .

As you can imagine, especially in a prison where there was heavy emphasis on **rehabilitation,** an inmate was smiled upon if he demonstrated an unusually intense interest in books. There was a sizable number of well-read inmates, especially the popular debaters. Some were said by many to be practically walking encyclopedias. They were almost celebrities. No university would ask any student to devour literature as I did when this new world opened to me, of being able to read and *understand.*

I read more in my room than in the library itself. An inmate who was known to read a lot could check out more than the permitted minimum number of books. I preferred reading in the total isolation of my own room.

When I had progressed to really serious reading, every night at about ten P.M. I would be outraged with the "lights out." It always seemed to catch me right in the middle of something **engrossing.**

Fortunately, right outside my door was a corridor light that cast a glow into my room. The glow was enough to read by, once my eyes adjusted to it. So when "lights out" came, I would sit on the floor where I could continue reading in that glow.

At one-hour intervals the night guards paced past every room. Each time I heard the approaching footsteps, I jumped into bed and **feigned** sleep. And as soon as the guard passed, I got back out of bed onto the floor area of that light-glow, where I would read for another fifty-eight minutes—until the guard approached again. That went on until three or four every morning. Three or four hours of sleep a night was enough for me. Often in the years in the streets I had slept less than that.

I have often reflected upon the new **vistas** that reading opened to me. I knew right there in prison that reading had changed forever the course of my life. As I see it today, the ability to read awoke inside me some long **dormant** craving to be mentally alive. I certainly wasn't seeking any degree, the way a college confers a status symbol upon its students. My homemade education gave me, with every additional book that I read, a little bit more sensitivity to the deafness, dumbness, and blindness that was afflicting the black race in America. Not long ago, an English writer telephoned me from London, asking questions. One was, "What's your alma mater?" I told him, "Books." You will never catch me with a free fifteen minutes in which I'm not studying something I feel might be able to help the black man. . . .

Every time I catch a plane, I have with me a book that I want to read—and that's a lot of books these days. If I weren't out here every day battling the white man, I could spend the rest of my life reading, just satisfying my curiosity—because you can hardly mention anything I'm not curious about. I don't think anybody ever got more out of going to prison than I did. In fact, prison enabled me to study far more intensively than I would have if my life had gone differently and I had attended some college. I imagine that one of the biggest troubles with colleges is there are too many distractions, too much panty-raiding, fraternities, and boola-boola and all of that. Where else but in prison could I have attacked my ignorance by being able to study intensely sometimes as much as fifteen hours a day?   ■

Comprehension Quick-Check

After reading "My Alma Mater," ask your instructor for a copy of the Comprehension Quick-Check Quiz.

Building Blocks

In each of the first four chapters you will find a section titled "Building Blocks." The Building Blocks sections are important because they provide you background information on vocabulary building and teach you strategies for increasing your vocabulary on a long-term basis. Read carefully each Building Blocks section before beginning the Vocabulary Activities for Readings A, B, and C.

Why Is an Extensive Vocabulary Important?

We know from research and personal experience that an extensive vocabulary is essential for several reasons. Probably the best reason was expressed by Malcolm X in the article you just read. Malcolm X wanted to increase his vocabulary so he could read the books that his friend Bimbi had read. But an extensive vocabulary is also important to your academic career. To grasp this point, read the following paragraph, taken from a college-level psychology textbook; then write a brief summary in the blanks provided.

> Freud conceived of humans as closed energy systems. He borrowed this theory from the principle of energy conservation. Entropy refers to the energy not available for work and, consequently, is cathected. In contrast is free energy which is available for other functions. If an individual is in homeostasis, then all energy is free and hedonism will accrue.

Key idea: _____

_____

Did you have a little difficulty in summarizing that paragraph? Even if you could correctly pronounce all the words, the number of difficult and unfamiliar words and concepts probably made the task of understanding challenging. Students with extensive vocabularies understand, with ease, what they have read. In contrast, students with limited vocabularies usually have difficulty reading and spend more energy and time on reading tasks. If you improve your vocabulary, as Malcolm X did, you should see an improvement in your reading and listening comprehension.

If you had to read and reread the psychology paragraph above in order to make some sense of it, you experienced what it is like to read with a limited vocabulary. Readers with limited vocabulary knowledge are typically slow readers. They may need to reread and look up many words in a dictionary. Of course rereading and dictionary usage are not negative behaviors, but overdependence on either can severely slow the reading process.

In contrast, readers with extensive vocabularies and background experiences are typically skilled readers who can easily make sense of what they read. Thus, a second reason why vocabulary knowledge is important is that it increases reading rate and fluency.

A third reason why an extensive vocabulary is important concerns the power and precision you have at your command for expressing yourself in speaking and writing. To understand this point, carefully read the following pairs of sentences, and check the sentence in each pair that communicates a more descriptive and vivid picture.

_____ The movie starlet strolled seductively into the room and impishly mugged for the press.

_____ The movie starlet walked into the room and posed for the press.

_____ My energetic pooch adores frolicking in the yard.

_____ My dog likes to play in the yard.

_____ The tedium of my history class was due to my professor's loquaciousness.

_____ My history class was boring because my professor talked too much.

The first sentence of each pair contains the more powerful and descriptive words. These words, in turn, communicate specific and precise images. The words in the second sentence of each pair, such as *walked*, *posed*, *likes*, or *boring*, are so ordinary that you probably received only a fuzzy or general sense of what the author intended. Dynamic and entertaining speakers and writers understand and use the power and richness of language. However, you need not be a professional writer or famous speaker to benefit from an extensive vocabulary. An extensive and rich vocabulary is essential for all the situations in college and in your career when you need to communicate effectively. The key to successful speaking and writing is to choose the most appropriate and precise word, not the most difficult.

Perhaps you are now convinced that there are many reasons to improve your vocabulary. With a greater understanding of words, you will be able to improve your

- Reading and listening comprehension
- Reading rate and fluency
- Effectiveness in writing and speaking

The next question that you need to ask yourself is what it means to understand or know a word. In the next section we answer that question.

What Does It Mean to Know a Word?

Edgar Dale (1958) suggested that word understanding probably exists on a gradual continuum much like the one shown in Figure 1.1. There are some vocabulary words that you have never seen or heard; some words that you have seen or heard but feel uncomfortable or unsure in giving their definition; some words for which you can give a general classification; and some words that you recognize and for which you feel comfortable providing a precise definition.

As an example let's use *engrossing,* a word used in the Malcolm X article. If you have never seen or heard *engrossing,* your understanding of this word exists at Stage 1. Students who avoid reading unless it is required by a course or professor probably have quite a few other words in this first stage. Remember—the more you read, the larger your vocabulary will be.

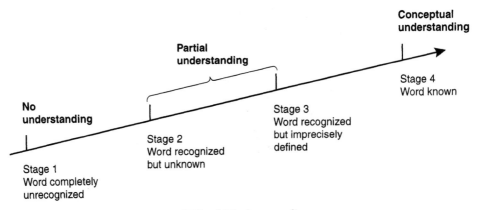

FIGURE 1.1   Dale's Stages of Word Understanding

Stage 2 is reserved for words that you have seen or heard somewhere but whose meaning you do not know. For example, you may have heard a friend describe a book as *engrossing*, but you did not know what she meant when she said that. Your understanding of the word is partial, though very limited.

In Stage 3 are those words for which you have some general, yet fuzzy, notion of meaning. According to Dale, a large number of words are in this "twilight zone"—words that fall between being known and being unknown. You might say, "Yes, I have heard of *engrossing* before—it describes someone or something in a positive manner, but I do not know the specifics." This fuzziness, also a partial understanding in word knowledge, can negatively affect your reading, listening, and understanding. For example, if you did not know the precise meaning of *engrossing*, you might conclude that your friend is describing the book as *engrossing* because it was short and easy to read. This interpretation, of course, would be incorrect, because an *engrossing* book is one that captures or holds your attention.

Knowing precise and accurate definitions of words such as *engrossing* occurs in Stage 4 of vocabulary understanding. This stage comes the closest to capturing what is meant by conceptually knowing a word: you understand a word upon recognition and can provide an appropriate and precise definition that fits the context. This is probably what you think of when you say that you "know a word."

Conceptually Knowing a Word.   Knowing the definition of a word is important and may be sufficient in many situations. However, memorizing and connecting a definition to a targeted word is only a beginning point. A memorized definition is often the tip of the iceberg, the part mistakenly believed to be the total iceberg because it is visible and obvious. Beneath the surface of the water is a much larger mass of ice, which is far more important. Conceptual word knowledge is like the iceberg beneath the water in that it, too, is far more important than the obvious dictionary definition. Conceptual word knowledge assumes that you will begin with an appropriate definition and then add three layers beyond that definition. Just as there is much more to an iceberg than what appears floating above the water, so it is with knowing a word.

Figure 1.2 illustrates the three layers of conceptual knowledge, or the rest of the iceberg. Note that the tip of the iceberg starts with a dictionary definition that fits the sentence in which you first discover the word. Words in themselves have little or no meaning. The meaning of words comes from the author's message and surrounding words and sentences. These pieces, put together, are referred to as the *context*. Hence, you will always need to select the correct dictionary definition carefully. In Chapter 3 we discuss this process in more detail.

Synonyms/Antonyms.   As Figure 1.2 reveals, the first layer of conceptual word knowledge beneath the water requires you to think of appropriate synonyms,

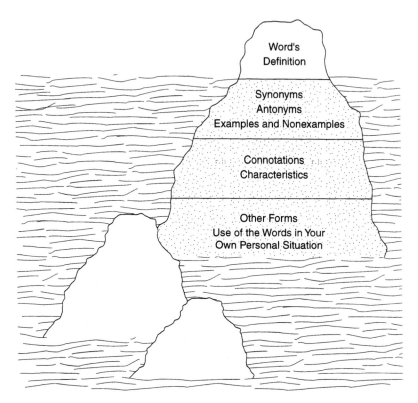

FIGURE 1.2   Conceptual Word Knowledge

antonyms, examples, and nonexamples for a word. A thesaurus and some computer programs may help you with this, but the best source for synonyms (words with similar meanings) and antonyms (opposites) is frequently yourself. For example, if your dictionary does not list an antonym for the word *engrossing* but you know that it describes something that occupies or absorbs your attention, then all you need to do is to brainstorm some words in opposition to the definition. Possible antonyms for *engrossing* might include *boring* or *uninteresting*.

Closely related to synonym and antonym knowledge is knowledge of examples and nonexamples for the words you are learning. Understanding examples that are discussed in the text and being able to think of others not discussed are both critical preparations for using words correctly in writing and speaking. To know that Malcolm X found books to be *engrossing* is an example from the text. But to be able to apply the word *engrossing* to your own personal situation is even more important. If you can describe a book or movie such as *The Color Purple* as engrossing, then you are much closer to a conceptual knowledge of the word *engrossing*.

Examples/Nonexamples.   Being able to think of examples or of situations that are not examples is also important to your word knowledge because it permits you to be more precise. This is especially true for courses such as sociology and psychology in which you are expected to learn long lists of key ideas. Many times professors devise test questions that ask you to apply a concept or key idea to a new situation. The following question from a college-level psychology test asks for knowledge of a nonexample.

Which of the following is NOT an example of hysteria?

    a. Being unable to hear anything even though there is no physical cause for your deafness
    b. Believing you are blind even though you can see
    c. Experiencing strong labor pains even though you are not pregnant
    d. Walking even though you are actually paralyzed

To correctly answer this question, you need to know that choice d is the nonexample. The other choices are good examples of hysteria.

According to Figure 1.2, the second layer of conceptual word knowledge requires you to understand a word's characteristics and connotations. The characteristics and connotations of words are rarely stated directly in a dictionary. Instead, they come from experiences with other people, reading, listening, and attempting to try out words in writing and speaking. Consequently, this level of word knowledge is learned not quickly or immediately but through repeated exposure to a word over a period of time.

To illustrate what it means to know the characteristics and connotations of a word, let's return to the word ***engrossing.*** After hearing and reading ***engrossing,*** you have probably determined that most people would like to be described in this manner. The word has a favorable connotation, and you would react in a positive way if someone described you as an engrossing person or said that a speech you gave was engrossing. In contrast, the word *dull* has a negative connotation. You probably would be displeased if your best friend described you as having a dull personality. Many words have either a positive and favorable or a negative and unfavorable connotation, and connotations may vary among individuals or across cultures.

Personalizing Words.   The third and final layer of conceptual word knowledge requires you to be able to use a word in situations and forms different from your first encounter with the word. This means you can apply a new word to your own experiences. For example, when you saw the word ***emulate*** in Reading A, you learned that Malcolm wanted to ***emulate*** or imitate Bimbi, a fellow convict. With this layer of word knowledge, you could apply ***emulate*** to your own life. Perhaps you have wanted to *emulate* your brother or sister because he or she has a successful job. Or perhaps your roommate likes to *emulate* or imitate the way you act in the morning after the alarm rings loudly. You probably have also asked your roommate not to *emulate* your grouchy morning behavior in front of your friends.

Understanding that many words can be used in different forms or functions is also part of the last level of conceptual knowledge. For example, *emulate* is the verb form, but it can also be used as a noun in the form *emulation* and as an adjective in the form *emulative.* In the same way, the adjective *engrossing* can become the verb *engross* or the noun *engrossment.*

> Malcolm X was so *engrossed* in what he was reading that he was angry when the lights were turned out in the prison.

The word *atheism* can also function as a noun in the form *atheist* or as an adjective in the form *atheistic.* The noun *rehabilitation* comes from the verb *rehabilitate.* After learning a word in one form, with the third layer of word knowledge you have the flexibility to change forms and functions to make your own writing and speaking even more interesting and precise. These layers, like the part of the iceberg lurking beneath the surface of the water, are extremely important for many reasons, the most important of which is to provide a conceptual understanding so that you can use new words in your own speaking and writing.

You have now completed the Building Blocks section of Chapter 1. We have described what it means to know a word conceptually. In the next section, Vocabulary Activities, you have an opportunity to work in more depth with the targeted words from "My Alma Mater." There are three types of activities for this selection and for each of the other readings in this book: Figuring It Out, Practicing It, and Applying It. In addition, at the end of each chapter you will find a section titled "Evaluating," which provides an opportunity to test or evaluate your knowledge of all the targeted words presented in the chapter.

Vocabulary Activities

 ### Figuring It Out

A.1 DIRECTIONS: You should be somewhat familiar with the 12 targeted words from "My Alma Mater." For the words you do not understand, use your dictionary to locate a definition that matches how the word is used in context. Then answer these questions.

1. What adjective with a positive connotation means the opposite of "boring or uninteresting"?

   _____

2. What word means "explained in detail"?

   _____

3. What word means "impossible to avoid"?

   _____

4. What verb with a negative connotation means "to pretend or to give a false appearance"?

   _____

5. What word means the opposite of "being active"?

   _____

6. What noun means the opposite of "a strong belief that God exists"?

   _____

7. What word means to "copy or imitate"?

   _____

8. What word means "new opportunities or new prospects"?

   _____

9. What word means "a proportional share or allotment"?

   _____

10. What word means "fastened and secured firmly or holding the attention of"?

   _____

11. What noun means "making new again or restoring to a former state or condition"?

_____

12. What word means "thumbing through the pages"?

_____

 Practicing It

A.2 **DIRECTIONS**: Read each sentence carefully. If the boldfaced word is used correctly, circle *C* and go on to the next item. If the boldfaced word is used incorrectly, circle *I* and then make the sentence correct.

C   I   **1.** After the athlete went through a ***rehabilitation*** program, she was able to jump without hurting her knee.

C   I   **2.** Sam's ***atheistic*** beliefs were obvious when he volunteered to say grace at Thanksgiving dinner, thanking God for the food and company gathered at the table.

C   I   **3.** The car salesperson ***expounded*** on the advantages of buying a used car from this company.

C   I   **4.** The movie was so ***engrossing*** that I fell asleep after the first ten minutes.

C   I   **5.** The secretary who constantly ***feigned*** sickness was given a raise by her boss for her dedication to her work.

C   I   **6.** Professor Miller's lectures were always so ***riveting*** that most of the students chose to skip class.

C   I   **7.** Traveling to foreign countries opens new ***vistas*** to anyone who is open-minded and curious.

C   I   **8.** If you avoid reading, it is ***inevitable*** that you will have a wide and powerful vocabulary.

C   I   **9.** After *riffling* through the magazine in the drugstore, James decided to purchase it.

C   I   **10.** Most little boys try to *emulate* famous athletes such as Michael Jordan.

C   I   **11.** The hunters were able to reach their *quota* of deer very early in the week.

C   I   **12.** The quiet man's *dormant* temper exploded when he learned that his son had been killed by a drunken driver.

 ## Applying It

A.3 DIRECTIONS: If you are able to provide a nonexample of a word, you probably have a good conceptual understanding of that word. Provide nonexamples indicating your understanding of the following boldfaced words.

1. Someone you would *not* want to *emulate*. I would *not* want to *emulate* a person who _____ .

2. Something an *atheist* would *not* believe. An *atheist* would *not* believe that

_____ .

3. A situation in which you might *not* need *rehabilitation*. You might *not* need *rehabilitation* if _____ .

4. An animal that does *not* go into *dormancy* in the winter. An animal that does *not* go into *dormancy* in the winter is the _____ .

5. A situation in which you would *not* want to *feign* sleep. You would *not* want to *feign* sleep _____ .

6. A situation that would *not* be *engrossing*. It would *not* be *engrossing* if ___

_____ .

A.4 DIRECTIONS: Complete the following analogies using the targeted vocabulary words listed below. Remember to keep the same part of speech across the analogy. Two of the analogies test your knowledge of synonyms, and one tests your knowledge of antonyms.

inevitable   quota   expounding   engrossing   dormancy

7. explaining in detail : _____ :: riffling : thumbing through

8. preventable : _____ :: riveting : boring

9. allotment : _____ :: vistas : new opportunities

READING B

Have you used your computer to make a hotel or airplane reservation? Have you shopped online for clothing or gifts? Reading B, "Getting Personal," describes some of the problems you may encounter from online shopping. As you read the article, pay particular attention to the boldfaced words. Before reading the article and completing the Vocabulary Activities, evaluate your present understanding of each of the 14 targeted words. Circle 1, 2, or 3 to indicate how familiar you are with each word (see page 4 for an explanation of the rating system).

Level of Understanding

alleging	1	2	3
amplified	1	2	3
conceivably	1	2	3
convened	1	2	3
desegregated	1	2	3
infer	1	2	3
meticulous	1	2	3
preconfigured	1	2	3
scenarios	1	2	3
scourge	1	2	3
surreptitiously	1	2	3

toting	1	2	3
trigger (verb)	1	2	3
unnerved	1	2	3

Getting Personal   *By Jennifer Tanaka*

Online shoppers will spend nearly $10 billion this holiday season. They'll surrender some of their privacy along with the cash.

If you're like me, the notion of personal privacy is lodged in the part of your brain where the fight-or-flight reflex lives. Privacy is something I think about only when I get a telemarketing call in the middle of dinner or a creepy piece of e-mail spam. Mostly, I take it for granted. I walk into a bookstore, toss down some cash, take my package and walk out. I assume that there's no way for the bookstore, or anyone else for that matter, to trace the transaction back to me.

But if it were an online bookstore, from a privacy standpoint, I'd be hosed. Going on silently, invisibly behind the scenes, is something called online profiling. It's a technology used by many of your favorite online destinations as well as the companies who place banner advertisements there. As you click your way through a Web site, a powerful software program running on a massive computer is watching and taking ***meticulous*** notes. Says privacy expert Andrew Shen: "The offline equivalent of online profiling was if someone was following you around the mall all day, keeping track of what stores you went into, what items you looked at and tried on, which items you purchased, when you entered the mall, when you left. Everything."

Online profiling may seem threatening, but it needn't force you to give up the advantages of e-commerce. Like most technologies, it has good uses and bad. Advertisers put a positive spin on the practice, saying it helps them to better target ads, so that relevant sales pitches may find their way to your desktop—such as a low-priced airfare to Hawaii while you're searching through a travel site for vacation bargains. Online stores say that it helps them improve the shopping experience.

No one is yet ***alleging*** that reputable e-commerce merchants are using this technology to spy on people or manipulate them—even in two class-action lawsuits brought this month against RealNetworks, a Seattle-based software company. RealNetworks has been accused of ***surreptitiously*** tracking the music-listening habits of its users through a program that 13 million people had downloaded for free from its Web site. Privacy advocates say that collecting data wasn't the problem; it was the company's failure to inform its users. To its credit, RealNetworks quickly issued an apology and a software fix.

Still, many people were **unnerved** by the discovery that the popular Real-Networks had the technological resources to gather the data without anyone's knowing. "Online profiling is just so invisible," says Shen, a policy expert with the Electronic Privacy Information Center in Washington, D.C. "Most people are not aware that this information is collected from them." And if you don't know it's happening, the thinking goes, you can't make an educated choice about whether you want give up your personal information in order to participate.

Data collection about your online behavior and personal identity happens in a number of ways on the Web. Most consumers understand that when they go to an e-commerce site and fill out a form (name, address, e-mail) those bits of information are stored somewhere in a database that belongs to the e-commerce merchant. How Web sites will use this information, as well as the below-the-surface traffic surveillance that might be happening, is what's supposed to be covered in its privacy policy. You can generally trust these policies, but watch for language that lets merchants change their minds in the future.

The real **scourge,** some say, is the data-collection practices of online advertising companies. The main way they get access to you is through the banner ads on Web sites. In a vast majority of instances, the Web site that you visit isn't the source of the banner ad that appears at the top of the page. Yahoo!, for example, uses a company called DoubleClick to sell ads into the banner spaces on Web pages. DoubleClick performs this service for more than 450 Web sites. Using cookies, tiny coded identifiers deposited on your computer's hard drive through your browser, DoubleClick builds a unique profile of you. Each time you visit a site that serves up a DoubleClick ad, your cookie profile is being updated.

The profiling is no different from what Yahoo! itself might be doing. But have you ever heard of DoubleClick? Or Engage? How about MatchLogic? These are all companies that conduct online profiling on behalf of advertisers and they know a lot about you. Engage CTO Daniel Jaye estimates that his company, just one of several in the industry, has unique profiles for some 35 million Web surfers, or around 40 percent of the total online population, stored in 700 gigabytes of data in a server somewhere. Each anonymous profile contains 800 "fields of interest" which **infer** your personality from your online behavior. For example, if you're someone who frequents recreational sports and parenting Web sites, your behavior suggests that you're a 30- to 40-year-old male with kids. This profile might **trigger** a banner ad for the new GM minivan—perfect, the ad copy might say, for **toting** around your kids and your team's softball equipment. Engage traces your exact footprints through a site but does not store that information in its profile database; instead it extracts a "score" that corresponds to a **preconfigured** field of interest. Nor does the company link personally identifiable information, such as names, to the profile. It also does not collect data on medical conditions, political persuasion or traffic through pornography sites. But could Engage do all of these things? "Absolutely," says Jaye.

Privacy advocates worry about potential abuse. The threat to personal privacy is **amplified** by the fact that on the Internet, previously isolated silos of data now can exist as a more or less **desegregated** information heap. Your marketing profile could **conceivably** be merged with postings you made in a newsgroup or open-forum Web discussion. "There's a push toward merging databases, and that poses new threats," says Austin Hill, a privacy fundamentalist with a knack for sketching truly scary **scenarios.** "Let's say a company says, 'We're not interested in having gay and lesbian customers, so let's not offer anyone with that profile this discount.' All of those possibilities get opened up."

EPIC's Shen says it's up to consumers to protect themselves. Hill's company, Zero-Knowledge (zeroknowledge.com), sells software that can cloak your identity—from others and Zero-Knowledge itself—while you surf the Web. Anonymizer.com is a popular site for doing the same thing, with a lesser degree of anonymity. Other simple rules: don't enter online sweepstakes; these are often fronts for companies that want to link your real name and e-mail address to cookie-based profiles. Learn about online advertising; 10 industry leaders have posted their privacy polices at net-workadvertising.org. Most important, read the policies yourself.

The Federal Trade Commission last Monday **convened** industry leaders to explain the details of online profiling. Afterward, chairman Robert Pitofsky says he "wasn't surprised" to hear that online profiling without consumer knowledge and consent was actually happening. "I had hoped that we would hear from the industry what their proposed self-regulatory fix would be, and that didn't happen," he says. Pitofsky says the FTC won't act until the industry submits a proposal. Profilers may be watching us, but now we are starting to watch back. ■

Comprehension Quick-Check

After reading "Getting Personal," ask your instructor for a copy of the Comprehension Quick-Check Quiz.

Vocabulary Activities

 Figuring It Out

B.1 DIRECTIONS: Using your dictionary to help you out if necessary, circle the correct definition of each boldfaced word. Before you make your selection, be sure to return to Reading B and see how the word is used in context.

1. "No one is yet *alleging* that reputable e-commerce merchants are using this . . ."
   a. stating and declaring
   b. guessing
   c. hoping and wishing
   d. trying

2. "The threat to personal privacy is *amplified* by . . ."
   a. suggested in conversation
   b. increased and made larger
   c. reduced or decreased
   d. complicated

3. "Your marketing profile could *conceivably* be merged with . . ."
   a. completely
   b. approximately in time
   c. surprisingly
   d. possibly

4. "The Federal Trade Commission last Monday *convened* industry leaders . . ."
   a. criticized
   b. elected
   c. assembled
   d. introduced

5. ". . . data now can exist as a more or less *desegregated* information heap."
   a. separated apart
   b. gathered together
   c. destroyed totally
   d. spread thickly

6. ". . . which *infer* your personality from your online behavior."
   a. declare as truth
   b. combine with others
   c. conclude from evidence
   d. perform as original

7. ". . . watching and taking *meticulous* notes."
   a. extremely careful and precise
   b. quick and speedy
   c. clever and brilliant
   d. useful and relevant

8. "... extracts a 'score' that corresponds to a ***preconfigured*** field of interest."
   a. unique and trend-setting
   b. after-the-fact
   c. proven before others
   d. determined in advance

9. "... with a knack for sketching truly scary ***scenarios***."
   a. movies about the future
   b. pictures with aliens
   c. outlines for possible situations
   d. stories about death

10. "The real ***scourge***, some say, is the data-collection practices ..."
    a. thief or criminal
    b. cause of pain or suffering
    c. interference
    d. confusion in a situation

11. "RealNetworks has been accused of ***surreptitiously*** tracking the music-listening habits ..."
    a. secretly
    b. openly
    c. clumsily
    d. enthusiastically

12. "... for ***toting*** around your kids and your team's softball equipment."
    a. working
    b. hauling
    c. planning
    d. suggesting

13. "This profile might ***trigger*** a banner ad for the new GM minivan ..."
    a. offer repeatedly
    b. reject soundly
    c. threaten or betray
    d. initiate or set off

14. "Still, many people were ***unnerved*** by the discovery ..."
    a. doubtful and questioning
    b. embarrassed
    c. upset or annoyed
    d. pleased and grateful

Practicing It

B.2 DIRECTIONS: Complete the following sentences, being as specific as possible in order to demonstrate your understanding of the boldfaced words.

1. The world-famous actor was very *meticulous* _____

    _____ .

2. On the way to school the child *toted* _____

    _____ .

3. I think I can *infer* from your facial expression that _____

    _____ .

4. The students in the auditorium *convened* _____

    _____ .

5. The salesman *amplified* his sales pitch by _____

    _____ .

6. The police officers were *alleging* that _____

    _____ .

7. The best *scenario* for your future would be _____

    _____ .

8. The argument between the players was *triggered* by _____

    _____ .

9. The students became *unnerved* when _____

    _____ .

10. The hungry dog *surreptitiously* _____

    _____ .

11. Most students believe the real *scourge* _____

_____ .

12. In order to create *desegregated* information for your research paper, ____

_____ .

13. *Conceivably,* the best movie of the year _____

_____ .

14. The floor plan of the house was *preconfigured* to _____

_____ .

Applying It

B.3 DIRECTIONS: Answer the following questions, making sure you provide enough detail to demonstrate your understanding of the boldfaced words.

1. If you were described as a *scourge,* would you be pleased? Why or why not?

_____

2. Would it be important for a thief to act in a *surreptitious* manner? Why or why not?

_____

3. If you were *unnerved* by several different questions during a job interview, would you expect to be offered the job? Why or why not?

_____

4. If your boss or superior *alleged* that you stole something from her, would her statement stand up in a courtroom? Why or why not?

_____

5. Would it be important for a politician to *amplify* his arguments during a televised debate? Why or why not?

_____

6. Would most students be excited if they had to *tote* a large book bag to school? Why or why not?

_____

7. Is it possible to *infer* someone's personality from the way he or she dresses? Why or why not?

_____

8. Do *meticulous* individuals have organized offices and desks? Why or why not?

_____

B.4 DIRECTIONS: For each of the following items, give an example that demonstrates your understanding of the boldfaced words.

9. A situation that would *conceivably* be horrifying to most people

_____

10. An action that might *trigger* a fight at school

_____

11. A place where people might *convene*

_____

12. Something in your home or yard that might be *preconfigured*

_____

13. A relaxing and pleasant *scenario* for most students

_____

14. A *desegregated* situation on a college campus

_____

READING C

What do you think of when you read the title "Sticky Stuff"? The sticky stuff described in Reading C is neither tape nor glue but the yellow stickies or Post-it notes you use almost everyday. In this article, you will discover how Post-it notes were invented. Before reading the article and completing the Vocabulary Activities, evaluate your present understanding of each of the 14 targeted words. Circle 1, 2, or 3 to indicate how familiar you are with each word (see page 4 for an explanation of the rating system).

Level of Understanding

amalgam	1	2	3
dubbed	1	2	3
debuted	1	2	3
entropy	1	2	3
foreseen	1	2	3
improvised	1	2	3
ingenious	1	2	3
invective	1	2	3
ironically	1	2	3
meshed	1	2	3
rendered	1	2	3
slathered	1	2	3
spawn (verb)	1	2	3
ubiquitous	1	2	3

Sticky Stuff
by Kendall Hamilton and Tessa Namuth

A tribute to three products that hold our daily lives together.

Never before in the history of humankind has it been so easy to attach one thing to another. Big deal? Well, consider ***entropy***. That's the scientific name for the tendency of things—atoms, molecules, paperwork, dirty socks—to become less orderly if left alone. Judging by your average desktop, plenty of people see nothing wrong with entropy. The trouble comes when you learn that scientists believe that as the universe becomes increasingly disordered, it runs down like an old battery. Not good. Fortunately, over the past century, inventive minds have brought us a bounty of products designed to keep our daily lives—and, who knows, maybe even the universe—together. The paper clip, for instance, is not only an ***ingenious amalgam*** of form and function, it's a powerful force for order. A few more of the finest:

Anybody who's ever struggled with a stuck zipper or stubborn button owes a debt of gratitude to Georges de Mestral, the Swiss engineer who gave us all an alternative. After a walk in the woods with his dog one day in 1948, de Mestral marveled at the ability of burrs to fasten themselves to his dog's coat and to his own wool clothing. De Mestral shoved a bit of burr under a microscope and saw that its barbed, hooklike seed pods ***meshed*** beautifully with the looped fibers in his clothes. Realizing this discovery could ***spawn*** a fastening system to compete with, if not replace, the zipper, he devised a way to reproduce the hooks and loops of woven nylon, and ***dubbed*** the result Velcro, from the French words *velours* and *crochet*. Today Velcro-brand hook-and-loop fasteners (which is how trademark attorneys insist we refer to the stuff) not only save the arthritic, fumbled-fingered or just plain lazy among us untold aggravation with our clothing, they secure gear—and astronauts—aboard the space shuttle, speed diaper changes and help turn the machine-gun turrets in the M-1A1 tank. Velcro U.S.A., Inc., engineers have even used the product to assemble an automobile. Try doing that with zippers.

Some theorize that the world is held together by Scotch tape. If that's not true, it could be: 3M, the company behind the brand, makes enough tape each day to circle the earth almost three times. This was certainly not ***foreseen*** by a young 3M engineer named Richard Drew when he invented the tape in 1930. Drew, who'd come up with the first masking tape after over-hearing a burst of frustrated ***invective*** in an auto-body painting shop, sought to create a product to seal the cellophane that food producers were starting to use to wrap everything from bread to candy. Why not coat strips of cellophane itself with adhesive, Drew wondered, and Scotch tape was born. It was also soon ***rendered*** obsolete for its original purpose, as a process to heat-seal cellophane packaging ***debuted. Ironically,*** the Great Depression came to the rescue: consumers took to the tape as a dollar-stretcher, to keep worn items in service. Ever since, it's just kind of stuck.

The Post-it note not only keeps information right where we want it, it may also be the best thing ever to come out of a dull sermon. Art Fry, a chemical engineer for 3M who was active in his church choir, was suffering through just such a sermon one day back in 1974 when he got to thinking about a problem he'd been having with ***improvised*** bookmarks falling out of his hymnal. "I realized what I really needed was a bookmark that would attach and detach lightly, wouldn't fall off and wouldn't hurt the hymnal," recalls Fry, now 66 and retired from 3M. Fry called to mind a weak adhesive developed by his colleague, Spencer Silver. Fry **slathered** a little of the adhesive on the edge of a piece of paper, and *voila!* He wrote a report about his invention and forwarded it to his boss, also jotting a question on one of his new bookmarks and pressing it down in the middle of one page. His boss scribbled an answer on the note and sent it back to Fry, attached to some other paperwork. Later, over coffee, the two men realized Fry had invented a new communications tool. Today Post-its are **ubiquitous**—available in 18 colors, 27 sizes and 56 shapes. Some even contain fragrances that smell like pizza, pickles or chocolate. Soon, perhaps, we'll have our notes and eat them too.   ■

Comprehension Quick-Check

After reading "Sticky Stuff," ask your instructor for a copy of the Comprehension Quick-Check Quiz.

Vocabulary Activities

Figuring It Out

C.1   DIRECTIONS: Using your dictionary to help you out if necessary, locate the correct definition for each of the 14 targeted words from "Sticky Stuff." Write the word in the blank across from the correct definition. Be sure to return to Reading C and see how the word is used in context.

Targeted Word	*Definition*
1. _____	seeming to be everywhere
2. _____	to produce or give birth to
3. _____	a combination of diverse or different elements or parts
4. _____	known or seen in advance or beforehand
5. _____	created or made without much preparation

Targeted Word	*Definition*
6. _____	original, brilliant, imaginative
7. _____	worked together, interlocked
8. _____	the tendency of a system to run down
9. _____	spread thickly, used great amounts of
10. _____	abusive language or insulting expressions
11. _____	pronounced formally, caused to become
12. _____	honored with a new name, named playfully
13. _____	in a manner that does not match what is expected
14. _____	made an appearance for the first time

Practicing It

C.2 DIRECTIONS: Read each sentence carefully. If the boldfaced word is used correctly, circle *C* and go on to the next item. If the boldfaced word is used incorrectly, circle *I* and then make the sentence correct.

C I   1. Because roses were **ubiquitous,** florists had to raise their prices for Valentine's Day.

C I   2. The unreasonable chairperson of the committee was **dubbed** "little Hitler" by the individuals working with him.

C I   3. The trendy art gallery refused to accept the painter's watercolors because they were **ingenious.**

C I   4. After listening to the writing instructor's **invective** about their papers, the students were thrilled and excited.

C I   5. The destructive hurricane was **foreseen** by several weather specialists.

C I   6. Trends in clothing are often **spawned** by singers who perform in videos shown on MTV.

C I   7. The overweight woman was told by her doctor to **slather** butter on her bread.

C   I   **8.** A fierce thunderstorm *rendered* everyone's computers useless.

C   I   **9.** Another television series about the supernatural *debuted* on Sunday evening.

C   I   **10.** Because the athlete was well rested and psychologically prepared for the competition, she was filled with *entropy.*

C   I   **11.** Guests at the wedding were an *amalgam* of relatives of the wealthy and influential groom and the extremely poor bride.

C   I   **12.** Because the hardworking student always prepared and practiced his speeches before class, they seemed *improvised.*

C   I   **13.** It was *ironic* that the movie about peace and love received such a violent and hateful demonstration outside the doors of the theater.

C   I   **14.** The two managers who dislike each other and have opposite habits will be able to *mesh* their work efforts rather quickly.

 ## Applying It

C.3 DIRECTIONS: Complete the following analogies using the targeted words listed below. Remember to keep the same part of speech across the analogy. Two of the analogies test your knowledge of antonyms.

entropy   ubiquitous   spawn   ingenious   meshed   invective

1. ordinary : _____ :: prepared in advance : improvised

2. to give birth : _____ :: to spread thickly : slather

3. complimentary language : _____ :: combination of similar items : amalgam

4. interlocked : _____ :: predicted : foreseen

C.4 DIRECTIONS: Answer the following questions, making sure to provide enough detail to demonstrate your understanding of the boldfaced words.

5. Would an athlete *dubbed* "Energizer Bunny" be suffering from *entropy*? Why or why not?

6. Would it be *ironic* for a lawn care specialist to have weeds that were *ubiquitous* in his yard? Why or why not?

   _____

7. Could a young child's *debut* in a musical watched by thousands of people in New York City *render* the child nervous or speechless? Why or why not?

   _____

 Extending

DIRECTIONS: Listed below are five words from Chapter 1 that each contain a prefix. Using your dictionary, look up the meaning of these common prefixes—*in*, *dis*, *un*, *pre*, and *fore*—and write the meaning of the prefix in the first blank. Then select a new word that uses the same prefix in a way similar to the targeted word. Write that word in the second blank. Finally, write a meaningful sentence using the new word in the third blank.

1. Word from Reading A: *inevitable*

   Meaning of the prefix used in the word *inevitable:* _____

   New or unknown word using the prefix *in:* _____

   Meaningful sentence using the new or unknown word: _____

   _____

2. Word from Reading B: *desegregated*

   Meaning of the prefix used in the word *desegregated:* _____

   New or unknown word using the prefix *de:* _____

   Meaningful sentence using the new or unknown word: _____

   _____

3. Word from Reading B: *unnerved*

   Meaning of the prefix used in the word *unnerved:* _____

   New or unknown word using the prefix *un:* _____

   Meaningful sentence using the new or unknown word: _____

   _____

4. Word from Reading B: *preconfigured*

   Meaning of the prefix used in the word *preconfigured:* _____

   New or unknown word using the prefix *pre:* _____

   Meaningful sentence using the new or unknown word: _____

   _____

5. Word from Reading B: *foreseen*

   Meaning of the prefix used in the word *foreseen:* _____

   New or unknown word using the prefix *fore:* _____

   Meaningful sentence using the new or unknown word: _____

   _____

Evaluating

Review and test yourself on the 40 targeted words in this chapter. Then ask your instructor for the comprehensive exam on these words.

Summary

In this chapter we discuss why learning vocabulary is important and what it means to know a word conceptually. As Malcolm X discovered in his homemade education, an extensive knowledge of words will improve your reading comprehension.

A large vocabulary will also increase your listening comprehension, reading rate, and effectiveness in writing and speaking. However, memorizing definitions is not enough. That is why we introduce the four stages by which word knowledge grows. A new word you encounter when you read or listen falls into one of these four stages:

1. The word is completely unrecognized (no understanding).
2. The word is recognized, but the meaning is unknown (partial understanding).
3. The word is recognized but imprecisely defined (partial understanding).
4. The word is completely known (conceptual understanding).

We elaborate on what it means to know a word accurately or conceptually. Conceptual knowledge includes the knowledge of synonyms, antonyms, examples or nonexamples, connotations or characteristics, and different forms of the word in new situations.

CHAPTER

2 Generative Vocabulary Strategies

DID YOU KNOW?

The word *prevaricate* originated from Latin and originally meant "to walk crookedly." Today, when you *prevaricate*, you talk crookedly or bend the truth.

Edgar Dale, in his article "How to Improve Your Vocabulary" (1958), stated that "the best readers usually have the best vocabularies." Although this statement is certainly true, many—perhaps most—readers skip over and ignore words that they do not know. Students tend to ignore unknown words for a variety of reasons, but the primary reason is that they don't know any *generative* vocabulary strategies that might help them determine a word's meaning and remember it for future use. The purpose of this chapter, therefore, is to expose you to generative strategies—strategies that you will use independently to increase your conceptual understanding of vocabulary.

In a sense, the vocabulary instruction that you are presently receiving in this text is an artificial situation. On initial examination, you probably noticed that the majority of pages in this book are filled with exercises designed to help you gain a conceptual understanding of words. The idea of what it means to know a word was explained in Chapter 1. This approach to conceptual understanding will help you learn new words for the course in which you are using this book, but in the real world, you must also think about ways to increase conceptual understanding of words in situations in which you receive little or no instruction. That is what generative vocabulary strategies are all about. The purpose of this chapter, then, is to show you a variety of ways to learn and remember new words as you read on your own. As stated in Chapters 1 and again in 3, you will discover that although looking up words in a dictionary may be a beginning, it is not enough, particularly if you wish to increase understanding to the conceptual level.

Research suggests that individuals who have read a lot have a major advantage when it comes to vocabulary knowledge. As Malcolm X discovered, the best way to increase vocabulary is through reading various types of material. Those who are well read regularly read magazines, newspapers, textbooks, novels, and so on. Note that wide reading goes well beyond comic books, beauty magazines, and the sports page in the newspaper! It's not that reading these types of material is bad—we consider any reading to be good reading—it's simply not enough in terms of both quantity and quality to have much effect on increasing your chances of meeting and learning new words.

Our message is that if you really do want to increase your vocabulary, and at the same time increase your knowledge, read! If you haven't been a reader, it's never too late to start. In this chapter, and in those that follow, you will be reading articles about a variety of topics. This diversity will serve as a vehicle for learning new words and concepts.

Now that you are ready to begin your new vocabulary-building program, you will need some tools to help you cope with the many new words you will encounter in college and throughout your personal and professional life. The Building Blocks section of this chapter explains some obvious and not-so-obvious strategies for learning new words and building upon them. In order to practice the generative vocabulary strategies explained in Chapter 2, you will read an article titled "Learning to Think," which contains 20 targeted words. Later you will encounter Vocabulary Activities, which will provide you an opportunity to practice your generative vocabulary strategies.

R E A D I N G   A

Have you heard individuals debate whether American schools are declining in quality? Have your parents ever compared the schools in your state with schools abroad, in countries such as Japan? Do you believe that Asians have better schools than Americans do? In Reading A, "Learning to Think," the author explains that Asians are very concerned about the quality of their schools and whether they are preparing children for the future. Before reading the article and completing the Vocabulary Activities, evaluate your present understanding of each of the 20 targeted words. Circle 1, 2, or 3 to indicate how familiar you are with each word (see page 4 for an explanation of the rating system).

Level of Understanding

amends (noun)	1	2	3
authoritarian	1	2	3
benevolent	1	2	3

culprit	1	2	3
deferred	1	2	3
disillusioned	1	2	3
elite	1	2	3
feudalism	1	2	3
glistening	1	2	3
hierarchies	1	2	3
ill equipped	1	2	3
innovate	1	2	3
plaguing	1	2	3
prodding (noun)	1	2	3
progressive	1	2	3
skimped	1	2	3
sole	1	2	3
steeped	1	2	3
stifling	1	2	3
torpor	1	2	3

Learning to Think

by Dorinda Elliott, with B. J. Lee, Barbara Koh, Jane Rickards, and Hideko Takayama

Asians are trying to prepare kids for the Information Age. Can creativity be taught?

Every year, as the rice seedlings first shoot up in Taiwan's ***glistening*** paddies, students make their final preparations for the university-entrance exams, and the horror stories begin. Sometimes, a body is found floating in the dirty urban river under a concrete underpass. Or anxious parents in a gritty Taipei suburban apartment find a suicide note on the living-room table saying, "I can't face the exams"; they run into the kitchen to find their son has gassed himself. Other times, parents can't be sure exactly why tragedy strikes: on May 6, Li Ying-chia, a junior at Minglun Senior High School in Taipei, jumped to her death from a tall building. She had been a confident, spirited student, and she left no suicide note. Though nobody knows for sure why she took her life, school authorities said Li had gotten bad grades on her practice exam. The suicides have almost become a part of Taiwan's rites of spring.

The deadly ritual betrays the crisis **plaguing** school systems around the region. What happened? Asians have always been proud of how well they educate their children. Thanks to the **prodding** of their determined parents, Asians score highest in science and math in worldwide comparisons. But from Tokyo to Taipei and Singapore, governments are realizing their children are so overstressed and overtested that they are **ill equipped** for the Information Age, where thinking and creativity hold a premium. Reform-minded educators share a similar complaint: ask a Korean student to write a creative essay or a Japanese student to pose a challenging question or a Hong Kong student to even ask a question and, more often than not, they will be unable to stray from the script.

Two years ago Kishore Mahbubani, a senior official in Singapore (currently ambassador to the United States), posed a challenging question at a conference: "Can Asians think?" It was a remarkable moment of self-doubt. For years, Singapore's leaders had been crowing about the advantages of Asian values, the idea that order in schools and government alike works better in Asia than Western-style freedom. But across Asia, that approach has produced efficient, obedient workers who let their bosses do the thinking for them. Governments merrily invested in production lines and skyscrapers, and even school buildings, but **skimped** on developing modern teaching methods and training teachers. The result: Asia's schools have been so neglected that in many countries, kids attend for half-day sessions in classrooms so crowded they are ready to bust. Asian students are too busy memorizing deadening answers to learn to think. In too many Asian classrooms, thinking actually gets in the way.

Many Asian governments have concluded that the main **culprit** is tests. In Taiwan, democracy has stirred public debate about the old-fashioned authoritarian schools, and by 2002, the government plans to abandon the **stifling** university examination system that has sent students into fits of despair. For decades, the entrance exam has been the **sole** factor in determining Taiwan teenagers' fate: students would prepare for as long as two years for the test by studying at evening cram schools. If they failed the test, no amount of good behavior in the classroom or hard work through the year could make **amends.** James Kwan, 19, was ashamed of himself when he failed the entrance exam last year. He stopped playing basketball so he could study full time for the retest, which he just passed. "It was really tough going," he says. In the future, university entry will be determined by a combination of tests, including one similar to the American SATs (Standard Achievement Tests)—which assess students' ability to analyze information—aptitude tests in specific fields and teachers' letters of recommendation.

Those reforms are stirring up a whole new set of concerns. Some Taiwanese parents worry that without a single standard test the system will be less fair. Some **progressive** schools are setting up committees of parents and teachers to oversee letters of recommendation and guarantee that connections aren't used.

South Korea has also decided to abandon its rigid university exam in 2002. But old systems, **steeped** in the traditions of **feudalism,** die hard. Despite the introduction of democracy in Korea, **hierarchies** still reign, and a university degree is the only ticket to a promising career. Korean parents still routinely try to bribe teachers with *chonji,* white envelopes filled with money. The teachers union, a pro-reform institution that has championed democracy in the schools, was recently legalized for the first time. Its leaders have campaigned against bribery, and the practice is fading. But without a standard test, parents worry that in the future, richer families or those with connections will have a better chance of getting their kids into university.

Educational reforms on paper don't translate into reality overnight. In South Korean classrooms, despite a series of plans to make teaching more lively, the **authoritarian** approach still rules. A middle-school teacher was taken to the police briefly last year after his students called authorities when he beat their classmate. A provincial education official recently handed out new guidelines: don't use sticks longer than 60 centimeters, use physical punishment only when other students can't see and hit people only on the "safe parts." Many Korean students go to cram schools or get private tutoring—and survive on as little as four hours of sleep.

In some countries, the computer seems like a shortcut to modern education. Malaysia launched an ambitious campaign, called the Smart Schools program, to introduce computers and the Internet into all its schools.

Hong Kong is still struggling to come up with a plan to improve its inadequate schools. Often, children under 12 get only a half day's education because of the classroom and teacher shortage. The government is investing in computers and plans to abolish the pass-fail university entrance exam.

It's easy to blame Confucius for the **torpor** in Asia's schools. Back in the fourth century B.C., the Chinese philosopher once said, "I transmit, but I do not create." In his view, the purpose of education was not to **innovate,** but to refine ideas that were developed in an earlier Golden Age. The natural order of the universe was based on hierarchy: sons respected their father, students **deferred** to their teacher and the people obeyed the **benevolent,** authoritarian emperor. Rituals dominated life, and rote memorization—and the ability to pass official exams—were all it took to succeed.

Asia's **elite,** of course, always knew it takes a lot more than memorization to make it in the modern world. That's why they send their own children to school in the West. Throughout the 1980s and much of the 1990s, the Asian boom was such a great party that nobody ever thought about the need to prepare for tomorrow. Japanese students may have suffered most from such shortsightedness. In the wake of Asia's collapse, they are so **disillusioned** by sinking expectations, rote learning and pressure to pass tests that truancy rates and violence are soaring.

Educational reforms won't solve problems like that without social change, from the sclerotic bureaucracies of Japan to the hierarchies of Korea's *chaebol.* As Asia's economies recover, governments will have to make hard choices. They can proceed without overhauling their social institutions, and continue churning out manufactured goods—for a while. But if Asians focus on the software of modernization, starting with the schools, they will rediscover what they always knew: of course Asians can think. ■

Comprehension Quick-Check

After reading "Learning to Think," ask your instructor for a copy of the Comprehension Quick-Check Quiz.

Building Blocks—Generative Vocabulary Strategies

Generative vocabulary strategies are strategies that you can use on your own to enlarge and improve your vocabulary knowledge. In this section you will encounter the following generative vocabulary strategies:

1. Context clues
2. The personal dictionary
3. Vocabulary cards
4. Mnemonics, imagery, and keywords
5. Grouping, mapping, and charting
6. Reciting and reviewing

After learning these strategies for learning new words, you should be able to choose an appropriate strategy, given your specific situation.

Context Clues

Probably the most common strategy or approach for students who have trouble determining the meaning of a word they meet during reading is to use context.

Using context means using the words, sentences, or paragraph(s) surrounding the unknown word to help determine its meaning. Sometimes context provides a considerable amount of information about the meaning of an unknown word; at other times, context gives very little information. It is important for you to be able to determine how much information you can get from the context so that you can decide whether you will need to use additional generative strategies in order to reach conceptual understanding.

Read each set of sentences below. The first sentence in each pair uses a targeted word from Reading A in a natural context; this sentence comes directly from the article "Learning to Think." The second sentence in each pair uses the word in an atypical context that provides much more information about the word. You probably will not encounter this second kind of sentence very often in the course of your normal reading.

1A. "But old systems, steeped in the traditions of *feudalism,* die hard."

1B. Today most European nations reject *feudalism*—an economic system in which lords had the power to demand work and respect from ordinary people.

2A. "It's easy to blame Confucius for the *torpor* in Asia's schools."

2B. A feeling of *torpor,* or apathy, overtook the college students after they took their finals.

3A. "Asia's *elite,* of course, always knew it takes a lot more than memorization to make it in the modern world."

3B. The *elite* players in basketball, such as Michael Jordan and Magic Johnson, will probably be inducted into the Hall of Fame because their scoring, defense, and leadership skills were rarely equaled.

The problem with trying to use context exclusively in sentences 1A, 2A, and 3A is that it does not offer much help. The problem with the second sentence in each pair is that the context is very helpful, providing information that would not occur in an actual reading situation. Although sentences 1B, 2B, and 3B are not very realistic in terms of what you might expect to find in actual reading situations, each one does serve to illustrate the types of clues that can help you determine the meanings of unfamiliar words.

Synonyms and definitions are the most common context clues. Sentence **2B** is an example of the use of synonyms to help define troublesome words. Remember that synonyms are words that have the same or similar meanings, such as *fast* and *speedy.* In sentence **2B** the comma following the word *torpor* tells you that *apathy* is a synonym for *torpor.* Sentence **1B** illustrates how writers often provide definitions within a sentence to help clarify difficult words. In sentence **1B** a dash is used to indicate that you are receiving a definition of *feudalism.* Since writers typically use a dash or a comma to tell you that they are helping you understand a difficult word, you should look for these punctuation cues.

Examples are also frequently used as context clues. In sentence **3B** Michael Jordan and Magic Johnson are named as examples of *elite* basketball players. As the sentence suggests, what makes these men *elite* are their skills and leadership abilities. When you add up the details and descriptions of Jordan and Johnson, you then know that here the word *elite* means a small group of the best and most highly skilled players.

Although you occasionally may encounter the types of context clues provided in sentences **1B, 2B,** and **3B,** you are more likely to encounter sentences like **1A, 2A,** and **3A.** In the latter sentences, the precise meanings of the targeted words are not provided, and if you have no knowledge of a word, you may have a difficult time figuring out its meaning, particularly a conceptual meaning, from the information provided. Nevertheless, because the meaning of a word always depends on the context in which the word is used, it is important to note the context, particularly if you need to pursue the meaning of a word by checking a dictionary or other sources.

"Learning to Think" is fairly typical of what you can expect to encounter in your everyday reading. As you read the following paragraph from this reading, be aware of how context clues do or do not help you to determine the meaning of the boldfaced words. Circle the boldfaced words that you believe have sufficient context clues in the form of synonyms, definitions, or examples.

> Many Asian governments have concluded that the main *culprit* is tests. In Taiwan, democracy has stirred public debate about the old-fashioned *authoritarian* schools, and by 2002, the government plans to abandon the *stifling* university examination system that has sent students into fits of despair. For decades, the entrance exam has been the *sole* factor in determining Taiwan teenagers' fate: students would prepare for as long as two years for the test by studying at evening cram schools.

How many of the boldfaced words did you already know? For the ones that you did not know, when did context help? What words did you circle? Let's look at each one and explain when context might help and when it might not.

In the case of *culprit,* context is not particularly useful. About the only thing you can determine is that there is some relationship between Asian tests and the word *culprit.* Context clues for *authoritarian* are also in short supply. You might guess that the word has something to do with being "old-fashioned," but that guess would not be correct. Without some prior knowledge of schools in Asian countries, you really do not have enough clues to determine the meaning of *culprit* and *authoritarian.*

Your luck changes somewhat with *stifling*. The surrounding information in the sentence tells you that these university exams have frightened students. In the next sentence you learn that students spend two years studying for these exams. Hence, by adding all the clues together, you could guess that *stifling* is an adjective that describes something or someone as being tough or demanding. The clues for the word *sole* also require you to piece together information, much as a detective would.

The point of this exercise is twofold. First and most obvious is that sometimes context is of little help, and alone it rarely provides enough information about a word for you to gain conceptual understanding. This is particularly true if you have no prior knowledge about the topic that you are reading and studying. If you have some knowledge of the word (perhaps Stage 3 knowledge in which you know *authoritarian* has a negative connotation but you are unable to provide a definition or write a sentence using it), context may provide you with new examples or details that add slightly to your knowledge of the word.

The second point of this example is to show the importance of looking at the word in a context larger than a phrase or even a sentence. Often, information that comes several sentences or even several paragraphs before or after the unknown word may give you more information.

Context is certainly important and should not be disregarded, but it is best used in conjunction with other generative strategies. One such strategy is using the dictionary.

The Personal Dictionary

In this chapter we are not going to describe how to use a dictionary; that is the purpose of Chapter 3. We mention dictionary use at this point primarily to alert you to the fact that a good dictionary plays an integral role in vocabulary development. As we have just discussed, context often provides only a few precise clues to the meanings of unknown words. Therefore, being comfortable with using a dictionary, and being able to use one efficiently and effectively, and in conjunction with context, is an important aspect of generative vocabulary strategies.

Since Chapter 3 focuses on dictionary use, our purpose here is to show you how to create a personal dictionary that might help you incorporate new words into your vocabulary. Included in your personal dictionary should be those words, encountered either in pleasurable reading or in course-related reading, that you want to remember and use later.

To start a personal dictionary, purchase a small three-ring notebook that will allow you to insert new pages. Divide the notebook in half, using the first part for general words and the second half for course-related or content-specific words.

Start with one page in each section for each letter of the alphabet. You might want to divide the content-specific section into subsections, related to the courses you are taking. After dividing the notebook into the appropriate sections, divide each sheet of paper by drawing a line lengthwise beginning about one-third of the way across the page, as shown in Figure 2.1.

Once you have drawn lines down several sheets of paper, begin reading. As you come across unfamiliar words, write them in the narrow left-hand column. In the wider right-hand column, jot down any information about the word that you might pick up from context. Look up the word in a dictionary following the procedures outlined in Chapter 3. Reread the sentence and select the most appropriate definition based on the way the word is used in the sentence. Try to generate several synonyms and write those down as well. Then, using context clues and the appropriate dictionary definition, in your own words try to state what the word means.

A couple of cautions are in order (we discuss them in greater detail in Chapter 3). First, when you are writing down the meaning of a word, be careful not to define the new word using another word with which you are unfamiliar. For example, writing down a definition for *indigenous* as "intrinsic or innate" would be of little help. Second, avoid using a form of the word to define the unknown word. For example, if you looked up the word *emersion* and wrote down "the act of *emerging*" as your definition, you would be gaining little information. What does *emerging* mean? Finally, be sure that you are writing down the correct def-

General Words	**B**
benevolent	

FIGURE 2.1   Page from a Personal Dictionary

inition of the word as it is used in context. The meaning of many words depends on the context in which they are used.

In order to let you practice making a personal dictionary, we have selected from "Learning to Think" three words that you may find troublesome: *glistening, hierarchies,* and *torpor.* Write these three words in your personal dictionary in the general vocabulary section. Then gather as much information about the words as possible.

When you reread the original sentences containing these words, you probably determined that two of them are nouns (*torpor, hierarchies*) and one is an adjective (*glistening*). For the adjective *glistening,* it is difficult to gain much contextual information from the sentence or paragraph unless you know what a rice seedling looks like when it first blooms. Hence, your next step is to turn to the dictionary definition. Be particularly careful to focus on dictionary definitions that match the way the word is used in context—to describe a rice seedling. A check of the dictionary will tell you that the most appropriate definition for *glistening* is "shining or sparkling with luster." Your personal dictionary entry for the word *glistening* would probably look something like the one in Figure 2.2.

Now write personal dictionary entries for *torpor* and *hierarchies* by using these steps:

1. Reread the sentence in which you first encountered the word.
2. Determine what part of speech the word is in that sentence.
3. Locate any possible context clues—definitions, synonyms, examples.
4. Check the dictionary to confirm your hunches from the context or to help you if there are not enough context clues.
5. Write your definitions in your personal dictionary.

Your personal dictionary entries should look similar to the ones in Figure 2.2.

Once you get used to using your personal dictionary during reading, reading without it will be difficult. In fact, eventually it will bother you to come across unknown words and simply skip over them. As your personal dictionary grows, it will also be useful in your own writing or, in the case of the content-specific portion, when you are preparing for tests. When you read, you can either look up words if you have forgotten their precise meaning, or you can add unknown words as you encounter them.

Vocabulary Cards

Some students prefer to make vocabulary cards instead of using a personal dictionary. Vocabulary cards are similar to the personal dictionary except that you

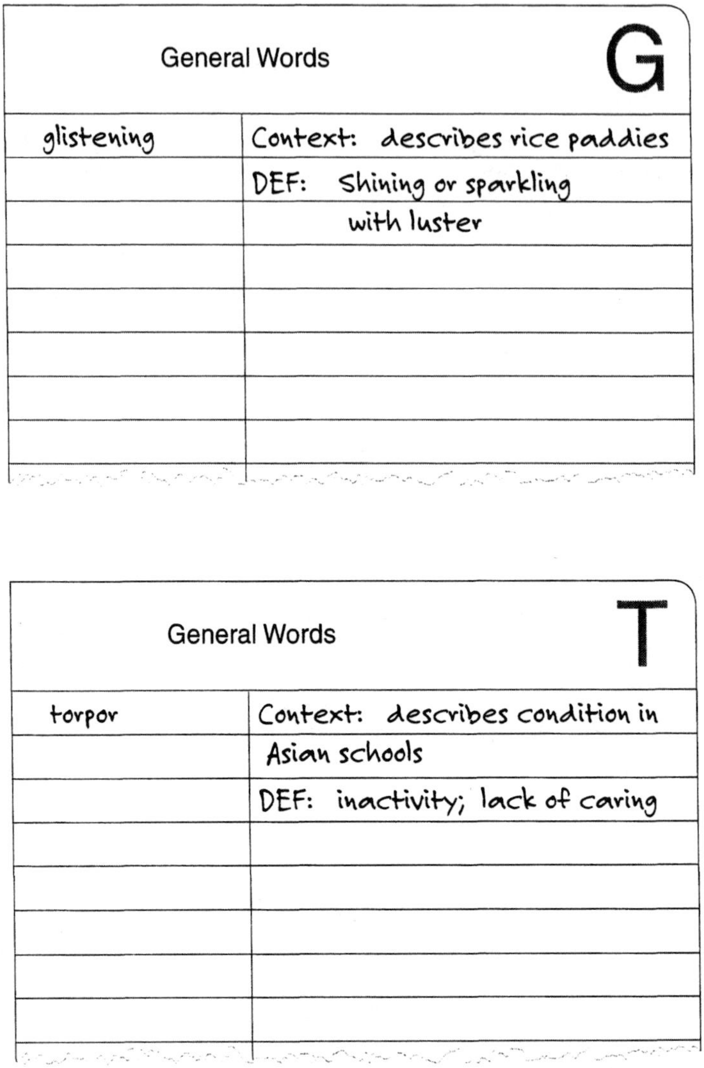

General Words	**G**
glistening	Context: describes rice paddies
	DEF: Shining or sparkling
	with luster

General Words	**T**
torpor	Context: describes condition in
	Asian schools
	DEF: inactivity; lack of caring

FIGURE 2.2   Specific Entries in a Personal Dictionary

use 3-by-5 index cards instead of a notebook. Like many students, you may prefer using cards because the words can be easily alphabetized and they can be tucked into a pocket or carried in a purse or book bag. In addition, you can group similar words together, or you can shuffle the cards to make sure you are not learning words in a specific order. Cards work particularly well if you want to make a concerted effort to increase your vocabulary and you plan to collect words for an extended period of time.

When making vocabulary cards, follow some of the same procedures out-lined for the personal dictionary. The first rule, however, is always to read with a stack of blank cards beside you. When you encounter an unknown word, whether in personal/pleasurable reading or in course-related reading, write the unknown word on the front of the card. After writing down the word, complete the card either immediately or when you finish reading. There is support for both ap-proaches. Making cards as you read interrupts the flow and can affect compre-hension. But waiting until you finish reading to find out the meaning of unfamiliar words can also cut down on your comprehension. Try both ways and see which feels more comfortable. A compromise might be to wait until you finish reading to look up words that do not hinder comprehension of what you are reading, but stop and look up words that do influence comprehension.

Once you have decided on an approach, complete your cards in the fol-lowing manner. First, if you have absolutely no understanding of the word (Stage 1), you may want to write on the front of the card the sentence in which the word was found, so that you have the context in which to begin thinking about it. Then go to a dictionary. Because many words can be used as several different parts of speech, find the part of speech, based on context, and write it in the upper right-hand corner. Flip the card over. Read the dictionary definitions, and find the one that best suits this context. Based on that definition, write a synonym in the lower left corner and an antonym in the lower right corner. More than likely, a dic-tionary will not give you a synonym or antonym. You will need to generate your own based on the word's definition. At the top of the card, write the dictionary definition based on the way the word is used in the sentence. Finally, if you can, generate a sentence based on the way the word is used in context. Remember, as discussed in Chapter 1, one way to tell if you are understanding the higher-level meaning of a word is by sentence writing. Figure 2.3 presents an example of a vocabulary card that could have been generated for *benevolent* in the article "Learning to Think."

If you are reading course-related texts containing many content-specific words, you might want to modify the cards somewhat. Figure 2.4 presents an example of a vocabulary card drawn from Reading B in this chapter. On the front, put the term in the center, the number of the page on which the defini-tion can be found in the upper right, and a mnemonic to help you remember the meaning of the term in the lower right. (Mnemonics, memory devices, are presented later in this chapter when we discuss imagery.) In the upper left-hand corner, include a piece of information that will help you group this card for future studying. This information can be a broad descriptor, as used in Figure 2.4, or a date or event. Then flip the card over, and on the back put the mean-ing of the term as presented in your text. If the term is not clearly defined within the chapter, check to see if there is a glossary that defines terms. If there is no

Front

Adjective   **benevolent**   Sent: Sons respected their father, students deferred to their teacher and the people obeyed the benevolent, authoritarian emperor

Back

DEF— wishing well on others   My sentence— The benevolent teacher always listens to the students' excuses.   SYN— kind   ANT— evil

FIGURE 2.3   A General Vocabulary Card

glossary, then consult a dictionary, but be sure to ask your professor about the term if it is still unclear to you. When you might need to know examples, include at least one on your card. For **hormones,** note that it is important to include examples of a variety of hormones. Often, however, no examples are given, even though you may be expected to know this information for a test. In a case such as this one, generate your own example, consulting with your professor and other classmates if necessary. Working through the examples encourages thinking about the term and helps you gain a more conceptual understanding of what the word means.

You can alphabetize, add to, and refer to these general cards during future reading, writing, and learning, much as you use your personal dictionary. You can use the content-specific cards to self-test text concepts in preparation for

Front

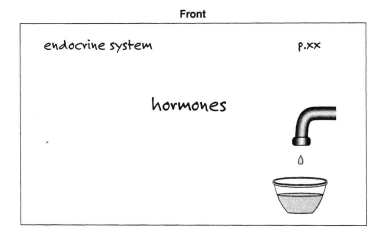

Back

DEF— An organic molecule secreted, usually in small amounts, in one part of an organism that regulates the function of another tissue or organ; produced by a variety of different cell-types.

EXS— thyroxin, estrogen, insulin, somatotropin, glucagon

FIGURE 2.4   A Content-Specific Vocabulary Card

exams. You can also group together like concept-specific cards. For example, you could make many cards related to different aspects of the endocrine system and then group them. In both instances, when studying, simply look at the targeted term on the front of the card. Then, without looking at the back, say aloud what the term means and give an example, if appropriate. Check the back to ensure that you were correct. If you were, go on to the next card. If you were incorrect, say the correct answer several times before going on to the next term. Always make sure that you say the answer out loud and that you can say the answer without looking before going on to the next term. In addition, once you know the cards from front to back, reverse the process. Read a definition and then supply the word that goes with it. Making and using course-related cards for study is especially good for classes in which many new terms are presented rapidly. Such courses might include biology, psychology, sociology, chemistry, and even art history.

Mnemonics, Imagery, and Keywords

Although you may make an effort to improve your vocabulary by using a personal dictionary or a set of vocabulary cards, there may be some words that you have a difficult time learning and remembering. Often, using an alternative memory device will help. *Mnemonics* is the overall term given to a variety of memory aids. *Mnemonic* comes from the Greek *mnemonikos*, meaning "mindful." We will discuss *imagery* and *keywords*, which are specific types of mnemonics.

Imagery is probably the most widely used memory aid. Put simplistically, images are pictures in your mind. Rather than remembering something through words as you might normally do, you remember through mental images. Imagery is best used for learning concrete words. Often, concrete words are nouns, since most nouns are objects that can be seen or touched. Some words, regardless of what part of speech they are, are more easily imaginable than others. For example, because the word *sole* is more concrete, it would be more easily imaged than *feudalism.*

Because imagery benefits some students more than others, try this experiment. Close your eyes and listen while your instructor, roommate, or friend reads the following passage. Try to imagine, or picture in your mind, what you would see and feel.

> It is an extremely hot summer day. You decide that an ice cream cone might be in order. You walk into the cool, air-conditioned store and decide that sherbet may be more soothing and cooling on this hottest of all summer days. Because it is so hot and you are so ravenous, you decide to have three scoops, each a different flavor. First, the server puts a large scoop of orange sherbet into the cone. Then he puts the lime on top of the orange. Finally comes the pale yellow pineapple. Your mouth waters! You pay for your cone and once again venture out into the dastardly heat. Your sherbet immediately begins to melt. No matter how fast you eat it, the sherbet, in rainbows of orange, green, and yellow, streams down the side of the cone, all over your clean white shirt, and onto the ground. You are a sticky mess, but it was well worth it!

How much of this scene could you image? Could you see the different colors of sherbet melting over the side of the cone? Could you feel the cool of the air-conditioning and the heat of the day? If you could, imagery is a technique that you should try as a way of learning and remembering new vocabulary.

In addition to devising images for words, you might also try using *keywords*. When using keywords, you think of a catchy sentence or phrase that is related to the word in some way. In addition, you can associate the word to yourself personally in some way. Personalizing keywords, as well as images, helps memory. For example, if you were having trouble remembering *obese* (or another targeted word from Reading B), which means "extremely fat or grossly overweight," you might think of the word as "O+BEES," which sounds like *obese.* Then think of an image that is associated with o-bees, perhaps seven very fat bees flying around. The bodies of the bees might be shaped like fat O's, as shown in Figure 2.5. This method helps create verbal or visual images to help you remember what *obese* means. Both examples use mnemonics and imagery. Also keep in mind that your mnemonics and images need to make sense only to you. In fact, the more they are personalized, the easier they are to retrieve from your memory.

Let's look at another example, using the noun *amends.* Remember that *amends* means "changes, alterations, or reforms." If you wanted to try to remember the meaning of this word using the keyword method, you might try thinking of *amends* as "a mend" or "a mending." Mending involves repairing a hole or a snag in order to change a shirt, for example, to a better condition. Many women used to spend considerable time mending clothes for family members. Thus, you could think of a sentence such as "My mother used to mend all my shirts in order to change or reform their terrible condition." Relating "mend" or "mending" to *amends* might help you remember the meaning of the word by using the keyword method without visualization.

FIGURE 2.5   An Image for *Obese*

Grouping, Mapping, and Charting

In Chapter 1, we presented the idea that complete word knowledge involves more than simply memorizing dictionary definitions or merely learning words in isolation. These activities often do not get at the connotation of words, which is important if you are to understand the conceptual meaning of words. (Connotation is discussed fully in Chapter 3.) At times, then, it is important to learn and remember how concepts are related to each other. In addition, it is often easier to remember words if they are *grouped and labeled* before you learn them.

Let's say that you have to learn the following targeted words from "Learning to Think":

authoritarian   progressive
feudalism   stifling
hierarchies   torpor
plaguing

You could arrange these words into different groups and then give each group a label. For example, *authoritarian, feudalism, hierarchies,* and *progressive* all have something to do with types of government or characteristics of a government. Hence, the label for those four words could be "types or characteristics of a government." Another way to categorize some of the words might be to group them according to the label "negative conditions or feelings." Three of the words—*plaguing, stifling,* and *torpor*—would belong in that group. Another way to group some of the words would be according to a negative or a positive connotation. Which words could be grouped in this way? Can you think of other ways to group these seven words? Keep in mind that the goal is to categorize words in ways that will help you remember them. Therefore, your groupings may be different from those of your classmates.

After grouping similar words together, you can use other generative strategies, such as vocabulary cards. Put your definitions on cards, as described earlier in the chapter, clip the cards together, and learn the words as a group, rather than in isolation. Once the words are grouped, it is also easier to begin to think about their connotative elements.

Mapping is another generative strategy. Maps are visual arrangements showing how words, ideas, and concepts are related. Because maps are advantageous for learning definitions of new words and for organizing numerous concepts and key ideas, they can be used in some of your courses as a means of test preparation.

If you had read "Learning to Think" as part of your assignment in a sociology course and you knew that you would be responsible for understanding the educational problems that other cultures faced and the solutions they created to solve their educational problems, you might construct a map similar to the one in Figure 2.6. The portion of the map on educational problems has been filled in for you. Notice that the other portion of the map, educational solutions, has not been filled in with any key ideas. What words could you use to complete the map? If necessary, refer to Reading A, "Learning to Think," in order to fill in the map.

For learning interrelated concepts, maps are probably more effective than the other generative strategies discussed in this chapter, such as the personal dictionary and vocabulary cards. The map shown in Figure 2.6 shows at a glance the educational problems and solutions in other cultures. However, not every group of new words lends itself to such a strategy. That is why it is so important for you to have a variety of generative vocabulary strategies for expanding your vocabulary knowledge.

Charting provides another format for organizing new terms, not only to learn definitions but also to see relations among concepts. Charting works especially well when you are comparing or contrasting concepts. For example, you could use charting if you wanted to visualize the similarities and differences between the various Asian countries in terms of education. As shown in Figure 2.7, the countries are listed horizontally across the top of the chart—Taiwan, Singapore, South Korea, Hong Kong, and Malaysia. The challenging part to charting is to decide what factors or characteristics to include on the vertical axis (from top to bottom) of the chart. In this example, you would list factors that help you understand the differences and similarities among the various Asian countries. Using the information from "Learning to Think," it was decided that those factors could be (1) educational concerns, (2) educational reforms, and (3) public reactions to these reforms.

Return to "Learning to Think" and see if you can fill in the chart using the information from the article. Are you able to complete the chart? One thing you might notice is that not every factor or characteristic applies to each topic at the

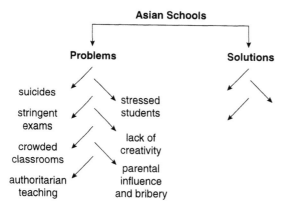

FIGURE 2.6   Mapping of Asian Schools

	Taiwan	Singapore	South Korea	Hong Kong	Malaysia
Educational Concerns					
Educational Reforms					
Public Reactions to Reforms					

FIGURE 2.7   Charting Reforms in Asian Schools

top of the chart—for example, you probably did not have any information about Singapore's educational reform in your chart. This is a natural situation with most charts.

When you create your own charts, you can use any of the following factors or characteristics for your vertical axis: (1) background information, (2) influences, (3) contributions, (4) beliefs or key ideas, or (5) disadvantages. Once you have filled in your chart, your next step is to study it. You can study your chart by covering everything except the characteristics on the vertical axis and topics on the horizontal axis. Then talk through the information, saying it out loud and, if possible, visualizing it mentally. If you forget something important, say it again several times, making sure that you can talk through and/or visualize all of the information without looking at the chart.

It is important to note that mapping and charting serve almost the same purpose. It simply comes down to personal preference. Both generative strategies help you see relations between and among concepts and are especially helpful when you know you have to compare and contrast. Try both strategies and see which one you prefer.

Reciting and Reviewing

One of the advantages to all of the generative strategies presented in this chapter is that you can easily test yourself if you construct the strategy correctly. Sometimes students make the big mistake of thinking they will recognize information when they see it. Those who fall into this trap generally do so because they opted for a short-term solution to learning terms and definitions and thus do not have a real understanding of the words. Memorization without understanding cannot stand the test of time, and students who memorize without understanding find themselves confused during exams and mix up words and their definitions. If you have ever experienced this situation, you have also experienced firsthand the pitfalls of using a short-term solution. In addition, those who use this method do not self-test in a blind fashion (saying the definitions, characteristics, examples, and so on without looking at the vocabulary cards) and often come away from studying vocabulary, as well as other materials from their courses, with the false assumption that they really understand and know the information when in fact they do not.

The long-term solution for learning word meanings is to stretch your understanding across the three layers of word knowledge. Multiple exposures to a word in different situations and in different forms, much like those you will experience in this text, will help you learn and remember new words. The long-term solution also relies heavily on recitation, rather than "looking at," and on blind self-testing. In self-testing, it is important to cover up the information that contains the answer. Instead of simply reading over your vocabulary cards or maps, you reveal only the keyword and then say the definition and any other pertinent information without looking at it. If you are unable to follow this procedure, then read the card or portion of the map several times to yourself. Try again, saying it "blindly" (without looking at it), and then check to see if you are correct.

Reciting helps to get the information into your long-term memory, and reviewing helps to keep it there. In a sense, then, reviewing is an extension of reciting. Once you have learned the words, the trick is to review them to the point of automaticity. *Automaticity* refers to the ability to recall something very fast—to the point where it is automatic. When you do something automatically, you don't have to think about it, like writing your address or telephone number. If you are learning vocabulary for the sake of learning it, rather than simply to do well in a testing situation, reciting should enable you to know the words so well that you can recognize them in your reading and use them in your writing or speaking.

In this book you will practice recitation, self-testing, and reviewing. These strategies work well if you remember the following guidelines:

1. Speak out loud, not silently to yourself.
2. When speaking, pretend you are giving a lecture to someone else. Try looking in the mirror or taping yourself for motivation.
3. When writing, imagine an audience. Pretend that you are writing to someone about the new words you have learned.
4. Conduct your reciting, self-testing, and reviewing over a period of time. Rather than spending an hour practicing 40 psychology terms, try five or six sessions lasting 10 minutes each over a period of two days.
5. Group similar words together to make learning easier.

You have now completed the Building Blocks section of Chapter 2. In this section, using the article "Learning to Think," we outlined and illustrated a variety of generative vocabulary strategies. In the next section, Vocabulary Activities, you will have an opportunity to work in more depth with the targeted words from "Learning to Think."

Vocabulary Activities

 Figuring It Out

A.1 DIRECTIONS: You should be somewhat familiar with the 20 targeted words from "Learning to Think." For the words you do not understand, use your dictionary to locate a definition that matches how the word is used in context. You may wish to make vocabulary cards for any words that you find especially difficult. Then answer these questions.

1. What noun with a negative connotation means "physical inactivity, apathy, or lack of action or caring"?

    _____

2. What noun means "changes, alteration, or reforms"?

    _____

3. What adjective means "singular or being the only one"?

    _____

4. What adjective means the opposite of "hateful or evil to others"?

    _____

5. What adjective means "holding back or smothering"?

    _____

6. What adjective means the opposite of "dull or lacking sparkle and luster"?

    _____

7. What adjective with a negative connotation means "not up to standards or regulations"?

   _____

8. What verb means "to begin something new or to create something fresh"?

   _____

9. What noun means "a small and privileged group"?

   _____

10. What adjective with a negative connotation means "against individual freedom or favoring absolute power given to one individual or group"?

    _____

11. What noun means "an individual guilty of a fault or crime"?

    _____

12. What verb means "soaked or saturated"?

    _____

13. What noun means "pushing or stimulating into action"?

    _____

14. What adjective means "advanced or moving forward with changes and reforms"?

    _____

15. What adjective means the opposite of "optimistic and filled with hope for the future"?

    _____

16. What verb means "gave in to another individual's wishes or decisions"?

    _____

17. What noun means "an economic system in which leaders rule over the common people and demand from them labor, goods, and total respect"?

_____

18. What adjective means "worrying, annoying, or distressing"?

_____

19. What verb means "was very thrifty"?

_____

20. What noun means "systems where people or things are organized according to rank or importance"?

_____

Practicing It

A.2 **DIRECTIONS:** Complete the following sentences, being as specific as possible in order to demonstrate your understanding of the boldfaced words.

1. After putting a dent in his father's new car, the boy decided to make **amends**

by _____ .

2. Because the participants at the party were in a state of **torpor,** _____

_____ .

3. In the United States the year-end holidays are a time **steeped** with customs

such as _____

_____ .

4. The chemistry instructor's **authoritarian** teaching style caused _____

_____ .

5. Because he was the *sole* applicant for the job, _____

   _____ .

6. The young couple decided to *skimp* on their wedding because _____

   _____ .

7. Once the *culprit* was revealed to everyone, _____

   _____ .

8. The young woman *deferred* to her supervisor because _____

   _____ .

9. The football players became *disillusioned* when _____

   _____ .

10. When the landlord saw that the apartment was *glistening,* _____

    _____ .

11. Many urban schools are *ill equipped* because _____

    _____ .

12. If established companies do not *innovate,* _____

    _____ .

13. The basketball coach *prodded* his players into action by _____

    _____ .

14. The private college was known to be *progressive* because _____

    _____ .

15. The instructor demonstrated his *benevolent* teaching style by _____

    _____ .

16. College students are often *plagued* by concerns about _____

_____ .

17. The numerous and complicated *hierarchies* in the office caused _____

_____ .

18. The young child found the church service to be *stifling* because _____

_____ .

19. *Feudalism* as a form of government can cause _____

_____ .

20. If a hospital decides to treat only members of the *elite*, _____

_____ .

Applying It

A.3 DIRECTIONS: Choose the word that does not relate to the other two words. Write it in the blank after "Exclude." In the blank labeled "General concept" write a concept or idea that describes the two related words.

Example:

<table>
<tr><td>funny
serious
humorous</td><td>**a.** Exclude <u>serious</u>
b. General concept: <u>characteristics of comedians</u></td></tr>
<tr><td>**1.** progressive
innovative
feudalistic</td><td>**a.** Exclude _____
b. General concept: _____</td></tr>
<tr><td>**2.** authoritarian
benevolent
stifling</td><td>**a.** Exclude _____
b. General concept: _____</td></tr>
</table>

3. disillusionment   **a.** Exclude _____
     amends   **b.** General concept: _____
     torpor

A.4 DIRECTIONS: Complete the following analogies using the targeted words listed below. Remember to keep the same part of speech across the analogy. One of the analogies tests your knowledge of antonyms.

    culprit   steeped   skimped   prodding   glistening

4. dull : _____ :: modern : ill equipped

5. soaked : _____ :: annoyed : plagued

6. pushing : _____ :: giving in : deferring

A.5 DIRECTIONS: Answer the following questions, making sure to provide enough detail to demonstrate your understanding of the boldfaced words.

7. If you were described as a ***culprit,*** would you be pleased? Why or why not?

_____

8. Are members of the ***elite*** considered to be ordinary and typical? Why or why not?

_____

9. Do most students enjoy the ***hierarchies*** that exist in college? Why or why not?

_____

10. If you had to ***skimp*** on your entertainment, would you be disappointed? Why or why not?

_____

11. If you were the ***sole*** individual to receive your family's inheritance, would your brothers and sisters be pleased? Why or why not?

_____

READING B

Do you wonder what kinds of food you should avoid and what kinds you should eat? Do you worry about the dangers of alcohol? In Reading B, "Vats, Fats and Rats," many of the rules about food and alcohol seem to have been altered a bit. As you read to discover these rules, pay particular attention to the boldfaced words. Before reading the article and completing the Vocabulary Activities, evaluate your present understanding of each of the 13 targeted words. Circle 1, 2, or 3 to indicate how familiar you are with each word (see page 4 for an explanation of the rating system).

Level of Understanding

admonish	1	2	3
ample	1	2	3
binge	1	2	3
bland	1	2	3
celebratory	1	2	3
enhance	1	2	3
hormone	1	2	3
injects	1	2	3
mimics	1	2	3
moderation	1	2	3
obese	1	2	3
receptors	1	2	3
voraciously	1	2	3

Vats, Fats and Rats
by Geoffrey Cowley and Adam Rogers

New alcohol and eating info may help set limits.

Who would have thought that abundance could be such a curse? Nearly a third of U.S. adults are **obese,** and the associated illnesses claim 300,000 lives every year.

Last week the federal government updated its official response to the crisis. Its new "Dietary Guidelines for Americans" offers the same *bland,* sensible advice as three earlier editions. But it also provides some small surprises.

Unlike past guidelines, the new ones specifically *admonish* consumers to limit fat-laden processed meats, such as sausage and salami. We're also warned to avoid heavily salted canned soups, frozen dinners and packaged snacks and dressings.

Vegetarianism was never mentioned before, but the government's experts now assure us that "vegetarian diets are consistent with the Dietary Guidelines." A meatless menu can provide *ample* protein and a full range of nutrients, the new pamphlet declares, "as long as the variety and amounts of foods consumed are adequate."

The biggest surprise involves alcohol. Whereas earlier guidelines denied that drinking holds any benefits, the new ones acknowledge that "alcoholic beverages have been used to *enhance* the enjoyment of meals by many societies" and cite recent studies suggesting that moderate drinkers have reduced rates of heart disease. "If you drink," the guidelines conclude, "do so in moderation." The panel defined *moderation* as no more than one drink a day for women and no more than two for men.

If Americans lived by the new guidelines—or the old ones, for that matter— we would no doubt look better, feel better and live longer. Unfortunately, when it comes to food, knowing and doing are different.

Picture this: You're a lab rat, *voraciously* chowing down pellets after three days without food. Then someone *injects* a chemical into your brain and, hey, you're not hungry anymore! You simply can't eat another bite.

This is clearly something we could have used at Thanksgiving. And, as it turns out, this could be good news for humans as well as fat rats. Scientists reported that they have discovered a protein that tells mammals' brains it's time to stop eating. Called glucagon-like peptide-1, or GLP-1, the protein is known to help digest sugars in the human intestine. But the rat study showed that after a large meal, GLP-1 is also released in the brain to signal that the stomach is full, says Donald O'Shea, a researcher at London's Hammersmith Hospital. It is almost certain, O'Shea said, that GLP-1 is in the brains of humans too. O'Shea and his colleagues reported their findings in the journal *Nature.*

The discovery follows several recent ones involving obesity. Last summer scientists found a *hormone* called leptin that may help set body weight, and two weeks ago they found *receptors* for that protein in the brain. But GLP-1, whose production may be triggered by leptin, seems to be the most potent factor yet. A pill that *mimics* GLP-1 could help people lose weight more effectively. But unless you're a lab rat, we wouldn't suggest a *celebratory* eating *binge.* Weight control is devilishly complicated, and any possible pill is years away. ∎

Comprehension Quick-Check

After reading "Vats, Fats and Rats," ask your instructor for a copy of the Comprehension Quick-Check Quiz.

Vocabulary Activities

 Figuring It Out

B.1 **DIRECTIONS**: Using your dictionary to help you if necessary, locate the correct definition for each of the 13 targeted words from "Vats, Fats and Rats." You may wish to make vocabulary cards for these words, using the guidelines presented earlier in this chapter. To complete this exercise, write the targeted word in the blank across from the correct definition.

Targeted Word	*Definition*
1. _____	uncontrolled indulgence in food or drink
2. _____	large or great in size or amount
3. _____	a substance formed in one organ and sent via the bloodstream to another organ in order to create chemical activity
4. _____	fat, overweight
5. _____	introduces or forces a fluid into the body
6. _____	not irritating, soothing
7. _____	reasonable limits, average or nonextreme quantities
8. _____	copies or imitates
9. _____	festive, joyful
10. _____	to increase or make greater
11. _____	to warn or caution

12. _____   nerve endings that receive or sense stimuli

13. _____   greedily, seemingly with no possibility of being satisfied

Practicing It

B.2 DIRECTIONS: Read each sentence carefully. If the boldfaced word is used correctly, circle *C* and go on to the next item. If the boldfaced word is used incorrectly, circle *I* and then make the sentence correct.

C   I   **1.** Everyone was in a ***celebratory*** mood after winning the state basketball championship.

C   I   **2.** James became ***obese*** because he failed to exercise during the winter and ate three large meals and snacks daily.

C   I   **3.** The strict parents encouraged their daughter to ***mimic*** the habits of the high school dropouts who gathered at the mall.

C   I   **4.** ***Ample*** leg room on the airplane caused the basketball player to feel cramped and uncomfortable.

C   I   **5.** The chef ***admonished*** his staff because everyone had worked so hard during the restaurant's rush hour.

C   I   **6.** The doctor advised the patient to eat a ***bland*** diet of fried foods, onions, and red peppers.

C   I   **7.** Older people often have difficulty in keeping their ***hormones*** in balance.

C   I   **8.** Organic farmers ***inject*** a lot of chemicals into their fruits and vegetables to improve their appearance.

C   I   **9.** People who love buffets and restaurants that have "all you can eat" nights tend to consume food in ***moderation.***

C   I   **10.** ***Bingers*** can eat entire cakes and quarts of ice cream in one setting.

C   I   **11.** The model decided to ***enhance*** her appearance by having cosmetic surgery.

C   I   **12.** After the serious car crash, the passenger in the front seat had no feeling in the *receptors* in his legs and arms.

C   I   **13.** After biking over 100 miles, the cyclists were tired and had *voracious* appetites.

 Applying It

B.3 DIRECTIONS: Answer the following questions, making sure to provide enough detail to demonstrate your understanding of the boldfaced words.

1. Would a person who *binges* on food be described as an individual who believes in *moderation*? Why or why not?

_____

2. Would most parents *admonish* their child for *mimicking* a barking dog during a church service? Why or why not?

_____

3. Do *obese* people usually consume food in a *voracious* manner? Why or why not?

_____

4. Do most people consume *ample* amounts of food and drink during *celebratory* occasions? Why or why not?

_____

5. Would it be possible to *enhance* your weight reduction by *injecting* a *hormone* into your brain? Why or why not?

_____

6. If you had extremely sensitive *receptors* on your tongue, would you want to eat a *bland* diet or a spicy diet? Why?

_____

READING C

What are your feelings about the role of prayer in the public schools? Do you know why prayer was banned by the Supreme Court? Reading C, written in 1962, will provide you with background on public-school prayer and help you understand the current controversies. Before reading the article and completing the Vocabulary Activities, evaluate your present understanding of each of the 16 targeted words. Circle 1, 2, or 3 to indicate how familiar you are with each word (see page 4 for an explanation of the rating system).

Level of Understanding

compel	1	2	3
conception	1	2	3
confronted	1	2	3
disgruntled	1	2	3
fervent	1	2	3
impose	1	2	3
martyr	1	2	3
nondenominational	1	2	3
orated	1	2	3
portentously	1	2	3
prerogative	1	2	3
plaintiff	1	2	3
recital	1	2	3
reverence	1	2	3
stringent	1	2	3
tumult	1	2	3

1962: The Court Bans Public-School Prayer

> Almighty God, we acknowledge our dependence upon Thee, and we beg Thy blessing upon us, our parents, our teachers, and our country.

"The Court Decision—and the School Prayer Furor," *Newsweek*, July 9, 1962, © 1962, Newsweek, Inc. All rights reserved. Reprinted by permission.

A thunderclap of outrage and shock cracked across the land last week following a U.S. Supreme Court decision forbidding the **recital** in New York public schools of this 22-word prayer to a **nondenominational** God. For pure **tumult,** the reaction was unequaled since the Court's 1954 ruling on school desegregation. It gave fresh evidence that nothing jolts many Americans more strongly than a challenge to the religious feelings which are still bound up with their sense of national identity. "Somebody," **orated** West Virginia's Sen. Robert C. Byrd, "is tampering with America's soul."

In ruling 6 to 1 that the prayer trespassed against constitutional guarantees of religious freedom, the Court dealt only with a particular form of public worship local to New York State. However, many **fervent** observers read into the decision a **stringent** new view of church–state separation that seriously challenged their **conception** of the role of religion in a God-fearing society. As Georgia's Methodist Bishop John Owen Smith **portentously** put it: "It's like taking a star or stripe off the flag."

Offense: The prayer which caused the clash dates back to 1951, when the New York State Board of Regents, the highest educational authority in the state, recommended that the schools, at their option, adopt an act of **reverence.** "We didn't have the slightest idea the prayer we wrote would prove so controversial," says John F. Brosnan, former Chancellor of the Regents. "At the time, one rabbi said he didn't see how anybody could take offense."

The school board in suburban New Hyde Park, N.Y., found the prayer equally acceptable and in August 1958 sent out a notice that as of September, the Regents' prayer would be used in local schools. There was immediate opposition from a singularly determined man. Lawrence Roth, father of two sons, one in the community's elementary school and one in high school, was disturbed by the idea that the state could **impose** any prayer on his children. "We believe religious training is the **prerogative** of the parent," he said, "and not the duty of the government." When a group of **disgruntled** taxpayers **confronted** the president of the school board, however, the official reportedly told them, "the board has voted on this. If we say it's in, it's in."

At this, Roth, who is vice president of a small New York plastics manufacturing firm, sought the support of the New York Civil Liberties Union, which was to spend more than $6,000 on the case. "A number of people had called us about the prayer," says George Rundquist, head of the state group, "but none wanted to serve as **plaintiff.** No one wants to get involved in a religious conflict." Roth, although not a **martyr** by nature ("I never felt I was standing alone, like Atlas holding up the world"), was willing to go to court.

Suit: Roth advertised in a local weekly for other parents to join him in the suit, but of the 50 who originally agreed to do so, only five remained by the time the trial started in January 1959. "It's foolish to get mixed up in an unpopular cause," suggested the employer of one dropout. Lower state courts maintained the prayer was constitutional so long as schools did not ***compel*** any pupil to join in over his parents' objection. A year ago the New York Court of Appeals sustained the order. . . .

The majority opinion, which put the Roths in the glare of national publicity, was written by 76-year-old Justice Hugo L. Black, who last week marked his 25th year on the High Court. ■

Comprehension Quick-Check

After reading "1962: The Court Bans Public-School Prayer," ask your instructor for a copy of the Comprehension Quick-Check Quiz.

Vocabulary Activities

 ### Figuring It Out

C . 1 D I R E C T I O N S : Before beginning this activity, you may wish to make vocabulary cards for the 16 targeted words in Reading C. After completing your vocabulary cards, answer the multiple-choice questions below by circling the correct definition of each boldfaced word. Before you make your selection, be sure to return to Reading C and see how the word is used in context.

1. ". . .prayer was constitutional so long as schools did not ***compel*** any pupil . . ."
   a. force or pressure
   b. reject
   c. increase
   d. discuss

2. ". . .that seriously challenged their ***conception*** of the role of religion . . ."
   a. birth
   b. idea or plan
   c. organization
   d. information

3. "When a group of disgruntled taxpayers ***confronted*** the president of the school board . . ."
   a. offered a proposal
   b. came face to face
   c. forced
   d. sacrificed an idea

4. "When a group of ***disgruntled*** taxpayers confronted the president of the school board . . ."
   a. important
   b. pleased
   c. angry
   d. loud

5. "However, many ***fervent*** observers read into the decision . . ."
   a. watchful
   b. quiet
   c. intelligent
   d. emotional

6. ". . . was disturbed by the idea that the state could ***impose*** prayer on his children . . ."
   a. suggest
   b. forbid or reject
   c. establish or force
   d. move quickly

7. "Roth, although not a ***martyr*** by nature . . . , was willing to go to court."
   a. coward
   b. politician
   c. debater
   d. sacrificer

8. ". . . this 22-word prayer to a ***nondenominational*** God."
   a. religious and spiritual
   b. without religious affiliation
   c. without names or homes
   d. reverent and sincere

9. "'Somebody,' ***orated*** West Virginia's Sen. Robert Byrd . . ."
   a. spoke in a formal manner
   b. chatted
   c. yelled into a loudspeaker
   d. whispered

10. "As Georgia's Methodist Bishop John Owen Smith ***portentously*** put it . . ."
    a. skillfully
    b. playfully

    c. angrily
    d. self-importantly

11. " 'We believe religious training is the ***prerogative*** of the parent' . . ."
    a. question
    b. right or choice
    c. burden
    d. enjoyment or pleasure

12. " '. . . but none wanted to serve as ***plaintiff.***' "
    a. supporting witness
    b. jury considering the case
    c. defense lawyer
    d. individual starting the case

13. " . . . forbidding the ***recital*** in New York public schools of this 22-word prayer . . ."
    a. silent reading
    b. musical event
    c. saying aloud
    d. invention

14. " . . . recommended that the schools, at their option, adopt an act of ***reverence.***"
    a. disrespect
    b. obedience
    c. organization
    d. respect

15. " . . . a ***stringent*** new view of church–state separation . . ."
    a. creative
    b. controversial
    c. severe
    d. logical

16. "For pure ***tumult,*** the reaction was unequaled . . ."
    a. disorderly disturbance
    b. quiet protest
    c. inactivity
    d. cruelty

Practicing It

C.2 DIRECTIONS: Complete the following sentences, being as specific as possible in order to demonstrate your understanding of the boldfaced words.

1. When you **impose** your values on someone else, you _____

   _____ .

2. A student might become **disgruntled** if _____

   _____ .

3. The **recital** of a speech might cause you to be nervous because _____

   _____ .

4. To **compel** their children to study, parents could _____

   _____ .

5. If you are the **plaintiff** in a trial, you _____

   _____ .

6. In a **nondenominational** church you would expect _____

   _____ .

7. **Martyrs** are individuals who _____

   _____ .

8. One should show **reverence** in church because _____

   _____ .

9. Wars are considered examples of **tumult** because _____

   _____ .

10. In America it is your **prerogative** to choose _____

    _____ .

11. It is often said that politicians are masters of *oration* because they _____

_____ .

12. When the baseball players heard the coach's *stringent* rules, _____

_____ .

13. The minister's *fervent* speech caused people to _____

_____ .

14. When the teacher *confronted* the child who stole the money, _____

_____ .

15. The student's *conception* about the chemistry course changed when _____

_____ .

16. After hearing the politician's *portentous* speech, _____

_____ .

Applying It

C . 3 D I R E C T I O N S : For each of the following items, give an example that demonstrates your understanding of the boldfaced word.

1. An occasion when you would state your ideas *portentously*

_____

2. A situation that would cause students to feel *disgruntled*

_____

3. A famous *martyr* (*Hint:* Think of someone who was assassinated.)

_____

4. An event that would cause people to act in a *fervent* way

_____

5. An occasion where *reverence* is expected

_____

6. An event or ceremony that could be *nondenominational* and an event or ceremony that usually is denominational.

_____

7. A situation in which your parents *imposed* a rule that you considered *stringent*

_____

C.4 DIRECTIONS: Complete the following analogies using the targeted words listed below. Remember to keep the same part of speech across the analogy. One of the analogies tests your knowledge of antonyms.

orator   prerogative   recital   fervent   compel   stringent

8. to suggest : _____ :: to avoid : confront

9. talking out loud : _____ :: conception : idea

10. one who speaks formally : _____ :: one who starts a court

case : plaintiff

11. choice : _____ :: disorderly disturbance : tumult

▶ **Extending**

DIRECTIONS: Most words have more than one meaning. Words with different meanings are sometimes called "multiple-meaning" words. You encountered several multiple-meaning words in Readings A, B, and C in Chapters 1 and 2. Some of those words are listed below. For each word, write in the blank a definition different from the one you originally learned. Then write a meaningful and original sentence that demonstrates your understanding of the alternative definition.

Example

desegregate

Different definition: <u>to abolish segregation, to integrate</u>

Sentence: <u>The public schools were supposed to *desegregate* in the late fifties</u> <u>and early sixties because of several court cases and state laws.</u>

1. dubbed (dub)

Different definition: _____

Sentence: _____

2. meshed (mesh)

Different definition: _____

Sentence: _____

3. triggered (trigger)

Different definition: _____

Sentence: _____

4. toting (tote)

Different definition: _____

Sentence: _____

5. riveted (rivet)

Different definition: _____

Sentence: _____

6. conception

Different definition: _____

Sentence: _____

Evaluating

Review and test yourself on the 39 targeted words in this chapter. Then ask your instructor for the comprehensive exam on these words.

Summary

In this chapter we discuss the importance of not only learning new words but also knowing and using generative vocabulary strategies. Generative strategies are those that you can do on your own as you work at enlarging and improving your vocabulary. Several strategies will help you with both general and content-specific terms:

1. Making the most of context clues
2. Introducing dictionary use
3. Constructing personal dictionaries
4. Making Vocabulary Cards for general and content-specific words
5. Using mnemonics, imaging, and keywords
6. Learning relations among concepts using grouping, mapping, and charting

We ended the chapter with some suggestions about how to recite and review using the generative strategies outlined.

CHAPTER

3   Dictionary Use

DID YOU KNOW?

The word *pariah* originated from India's caste system. The lowest caste, or group, was hired to beat drums, or **parai**, at certain festivals. Today the word *pariah* means any despised person or outcast.

Every vocabulary book offers advice about how to use a dictionary. Although this book is obviously not an exception to the rule, we do offer a less traditional approach to many aspects of dictionary use. We assume, for example, that since you are in college, you have had a considerable amount of experience looking up words in a dictionary. Therefore, we spend only a small amount of time discussing dictionary entries, guide words, and the like. Rather, in most of this chapter we offer suggestions that might help you realize the benefits of dictionary use, and help you use a dictionary more as a learning tool than as a single source for learning all unknown words. In the Building Blocks section of this chapter, we discuss five issues relating to the dictionary: (1) identifying effective definitions, or word denotation; (2) interpreting dictionary entries; (3) describing word etymologies and word origins; (4) understanding word connotations, or the more experiential part of learning words; and (5) combining both context and dictionary use to learn new words.

It may come as a surprise to you to learn that, at best, dictionaries often offer limited assistance in learning unknown words. Elements of practicality must be taken into consideration when compiling a dictionary. One element is that lexicographers (individuals who compile dictionaries) are obviously limited by space. Current standard dictionaries have over 200,000 entries. If lexicographers wrote explicit and strong definitions for all of them, such a dictionary would be so large that few people would be able to lift it, and so expensive that few could afford to buy it. As a result, some dictionary entries are fairly strong and useful, but others are less helpful.

READING A

In order to make this chapter as practical as possible, we include as Reading A a magazine excerpt entitled "A Bigger Hole in the Ozone." This selection contains numerous words that we will discuss as we present information about the denotation and connotation of words. Before reading the article and completing the Vocabulary Activities, evaluate your present understanding of each of the 14 targeted words. Circle 1, 2, or 3 to indicate how familiar you are with each word (see page 4 for an explanation of the rating system).

Level of Understanding

anchors (verb)	1	2	3
benign	1	2	3
chlorofluorocarbons	1	2	3
conservative	1	2	3
cripple	1	2	3
endangered	1	2	3
fatality	1	2	3
forecast	1	2	3
graver	1	2	3
incidence	1	2	3
intensify	1	2	3
regulators	1	2	3
solvents	1	2	3
stratosphere	1	2	3

A Bigger Hole in the Ozone   *by Sharon Begley*

EPA Predicts 200,000 More Skin-Cancer Deaths: The nations of the world have never agreed on how to halt the destruction of rain forests or save *endangered* species. But when it came to saving the ozone layer, which screens out the sun's harmful ultraviolet rays, they knew just what to do. Or so it seemed. In 1987, 24 nations meeting in Montreal pledged that, by the year 2000, they would halve their production of **chlorofluorocarbons** (CFCs), chemicals that destroy ozone. That was when the only ozone hole that had been noticed was over Antarctica. But soon after, satellite data showed that ozone above the United States had dropped 1.5 percent. That persuaded more than 90 countries last June to agree to ban CFCs entirely by 2000. Developing nations were given until 2010 to stop producing ozone-damaging chemicals; wealthier countries promised them up to $240 million to help make the switch.

Now it seems that the problem is far **graver** than anyone thought. Environmental Protection Agency chief William Reilly announced that ozone loss over the United States since 1978 has amounted to a "stunning" 4 to 5 percent. The preliminary satellite data, which scientists have been analyzing since last autumn, show that Europe, the Soviet Union and northern Asia experienced similar losses, while areas at the latitude of Sweden and Hudson Bay saw losses of 8 percent. "Past studies had shown about half that amount," said Reilly. "As a result, there could be 200,000 deaths from skin cancer in the United States over the next 50 years" in addition to the 400,000 otherwise expected over that period. The **fatality** estimate was 21 times what the EPA had **forecast** earlier. Ultraviolet radiation can also cause cataracts, weaken the immune system, damage crops and disrupt the reproduction of plankton that **anchors** the marine food chain.

Danger: Sunlight

- Every 1 percent drop in ozone allows 2 percent more ultraviolet light to reach Earth's surface.
- Every 1 percent reduction in ozone raises the **incidence** of skin cancer by 5 to 7 percent.
- The 5 percent loss of ozone over the U.S. is expected to cause 4,000 more skin-cancer deaths a year.
- The ozone loss is greater at higher latitudes. Over Leningrad, it is as much as 8 percent.

And the ozone loss is almost certain to get worse. CFCs stay in the atmosphere for decades. The EPA's Eileen Claussen told *Newsweek* that the agency's models show ozone loss of 10 to 12 percent over the next 20 years—"and we've already thrown out those estimates because they are far too **conservative**."

Reilly vowed that the EPA would **intensify** its efforts to find substitutes for ozone-eating substances. Researchers have made progress in finding **benign** chemicals that do the job of chlorine-based **solvents,** but they have been less successful in replacing the CFCs used in refrigerators and air conditioners. If substitute chemicals can be found, developing nations might be persuaded to phase out CFCs by 2000 rather than 2010. Right now, countries such as China and India believe that abandoning CFCs too quickly would ***cripple*** their economies. Eliminating CFCs before 2000, though, would not make much difference, because so many of the chemicals are already on their way to the ***stratosphere.*** In effect, ***regulators*** are running out of ideas. "Because such aggressive steps have already been taken," Claussen says, "it's hard to come up with anything more that can make a difference." ■

Comprehension Quick-Check

After reading "A Bigger Hole in the Ozone," ask your instructor for a copy of the Comprehension Quick-Check Quiz.

Building Blocks

Denotation: Effective and Less Effective Dictionary Definitions

Although dictionaries can be used for many purposes, their main function is to provide denotations, or definitions, of words. But not all definitions are created equal. To get an idea of the difference between strong and weak dictionary entries, we'll look at several examples.

The following sentence comes from Reading A, the article you just read:

The nations of the world have never agreed on how to halt the destruction of rain forests or save ***endangered*** species.

In this sentence, unless you already know the meaning of ***endangered*** the context fails to provide much assistance as to its meaning. So, as a conscientious student, you turn to a dictionary for a definition. But the entry for ***endangered*** reads like this:

en•dan•gered (ĕn-dān′jərd) *adj.* Faced with extinction.

The dictionary definition provides little help unless you know the meaning of *extinction,* so you are left frustrated because neither context nor the dictionary gives enough assistance for you to gain even partial word knowledge.

Definitions copyright © 1996 by Houghton Mifflin Company. Reproduced by permission from *The American Heritage Dictionary of the English Language, Third Edition.*

Now, let's examine an example from Reading A for which the dictionary may be somewhat more friendly and effective:

Every 1 percent reduction in ozone raises the *incidence* of skin cancer by 5 to 7 percent.

You get a vague idea of the meaning of *incidence* through context, but you still may feel the need for a clear and precise dictionary definition. When you look up *incidence,* you are given the following definitions:

> in•ci•dence (ĭn′sĭ-dəns) *n.* **1.** the act or an instance of happening; occurrence. **2.** Extent or frequency of occurrence: *high incidence of malaria.* **3.** *Phys.* **a.** The arrival of radiation or a projectile at a surface. **b.** Angle of incidence.

This entry is much clearer and is easier to understand, but you still must be able to select the definition that fits the context. It is easy to eliminate definition 3 since the sentence has nothing to do with physics. The example in definition 2 is directly related to how the word *incidence* is used in the article. The example mentions the "high *incidence* of malaria" or the frequency of malaria, and the article talks about the "*incidence* of skin cancer" or the frequency of skin cancer.

Those two very different examples of dictionary entries show that some definitions are better and stronger than others.

Let's examine one more example. The following sentence is also from Reading A:

Now it seems that the problem is far *graver* than anyone thought.

When you look up the word *grave,* you are faced with a laundry list of definitions:

> grave¹ (grāv) *n.* **1.a.** An excavation for the interment of a corpse. **b.** A place of burial. **2.** Death or extinction [ME < OE *græf.* See **ghrebh-2***.]
>
> grave² (grāv) *adj.* grav•er, grav•est. **1.** Requiring serious thought; momentous. **2.** Fraught with danger or harm. **3.** Dignified and somber in conduct or character. See synonym **serious. 4.** Somber or dark in hue. **5.** (also gräv). *Lang.* **a.** Written with or modified by the mark (`), as the è in Sèvres. **b.** Of or referring to a phonetic feature that distinguishes sounds made at the periphery of the vocal tract, as in labial consonants and back vowels. [Fr. < OFr. < Lat. *gravis* See **gʷerə-1***.] — **grave′ly** *adv.* — **grave′ness** *n.*
>
> grave³ (grāv) *tr.v.* graved, grav•en (grā′vən) or graved, graving, graves. **1.** To sculpt or carve; engrave. **2.** To stamp or impress deeply; fix permanently. [ME *graven* < OE *grafan* See **ghrebh-2***.]
>
> grave⁴ (grāv) *tr.v.* graved, grav•ing, graves. To clean and coat (the bottom of a wooden ship) with pitch. [ME *graven.*]
>
> gra•ve⁵ (grä′vā) *adv. & adj. Mus.* In a slow and solemn manner. [Ital. < Lat. *gravis,* heavy. See GRAVE².]

However, only definition 2 includes the word *graver,* an adjective. This narrows your search somewhat, but you are still faced with five slightly different definitions in definition 2 alone. Reread the example sentence. Which definition from definition 2 makes the most sense in this context: "the problem is far *graver*"? The second definition seems to fit this context best, but finding this definition takes some thought and effort.

Characteristics of Effective Definitions. To make the best use of a dictionary, you need to understand that some definitions are clearer and better than others, thus do a better job of enhancing denotative word knowledge. The most effective dictionary definitions have the following five characteristics (adapted from McKeown, 1990):

1. The definition does not contain another form of the word being defined. For example, defining ***regulator*** as "one that regulates" would give virtually no information about the meaning of the word. Such a definition would be very ineffective.
2. The definition uses precise language that has a high degree of explaining power. Vague language often fails to convey the meaning of the word. The first definition of ***incidence*** offers a good example of vague language. *Act, instance,* and *happening* are all vague words.
3. The definition is written in such a way that readers are not likely to substitute an incorrect synonym for the word being defined. Suppose the word *adamant* is defined as "a legendary stone believed to be impenetrable" or "an extremely hard substance." The definition provides no information about what can or cannot be *adamant,* and it encourages the reader to substitute *hard* for *adamant* and write an incorrect sentence such as the following:

   Automobiles are made of *adamant* substances that are not easily damaged.

   When used as an adjective, *adamant* actually means "unyielding or firm" and usually has to do with abstractions such as beliefs or opinions. The following sentence uses the word correctly:

   Although most of her friends disagreed, June was *adamant* in her beliefs on certain environmental issues.

4. A definition that provides multiple pieces of information also offers some guidance about how to integrate these pieces of information. For the word *chronic,* the following entry is provided:

   chron•ic (krŏn′ĭk) *adj.* **1.** Of long duration; continuing: *chronic problems.* **2.** Lasting for a long period of time or marked by frequent recurrence: *chronic colitis.* **3.** Subject to a habit or pattern of behavior for a long time. [Fr. *chronique* < Lat.

chronicus < Gk. *khronikos,* of time < *khronos,* time. — **chron′i•cal•ly** *adv.* — **chro•nic′i•ty** (krŏ-nĭs´ ĭ-tē) *n.*

Note that although several pieces of information are given, the entry does provide guidance concerning when they might be appropriate. The entry states that something *chronic* can be "of long duration; continuing," and also offers "*chronic problems*" to indicate something that can be *chronic.*

5. A definition provides examples, when necessary, so that readers can see proper usage of the word, particularly in situations in which it may be easy to misinterpret the stated definition. The definition of *chronic* gives examples of correct context: "*chronic colitis*" and "*chronic problems*" extend dictionary understanding.

Only rarely does a definition possess all five characteristics. A moderately effective definition might have two or three of the characteristics. A less effective definition might have only one or, in some cases, none.

As you can see, dictionaries provide a wide range of definition levels. But they also provide information beyond the meaning of the word. Now that you have an idea about the characteristics of effective and less effective definitions, let's progress a step further and examine the other information that dictionary entries supply.

Making Sense of Dictionary Entries

Although dictionary definitions are not perfect, they can be an excellent starting point for understanding a word. You must, however, know how to interpret an entry so that you will be able to select the most appropriate definition. As mentioned in Chapter 1, words rarely exist and have meaning in isolation; instead, they gather meaning from surrounding words and sentences. Consequently, the first listed dictionary definition might not be the most appropriate. You will have to read all the entries before making a judgment.

In this section, we will help you in the selection process by explaining the typical entry pattern of one dictionary, *The American Heritage College Dictionary, Third Edition.* In fact, we will be using this dictionary throughout the book as our guide to words and their definitions.

A word of caution is in order about the role of synonym/antonym books, thesauruses, and computer synonym/antonym programs. Most pocket computer dictionaries also require this cautionary note. Tools such as these, though appropriate in some instances, are generally inappropriate for gaining a conceptual understanding of words. They probably work best when you already have a fair understanding of a word but perhaps need another word to take its place or contrast with it. For example, if you were writing a paper and used the word *ample* to describe the average salary of a CEO and then wanted to use another word with a similar meaning later in the paper, you might refer to a thesaurus, synonym/antonym book, or a computerized dictionary. But if you thought that *ample* might be a good word to describe salaries and you were not sure of its exact meaning, you would want to consult a dictionary or perhaps use one of your generative vocabulary strategies in order to understand it better.

The point we want to stress here is that the tools you use to learn vocabulary should fit the situation in which you find yourself. We find that students often consult a thesaurus and then replace one word that they don't understand very well with another word that they know even less well! In this situation, more often than not, the word is used incorrectly. What you should be able to do after learning about the different generative strategies for learning new words is to choose the appropriate tools for your specific situation.

Rather than practice dictionary entry skills in a series of drills, you will work with some targeted words from Reading A, "A Bigger Hole in the Ozone." If some time has passed since you read this article, review it now to refresh your memory before going on to the next section.

Interpreting a Typical Entry.   Dictionary entries for *fatality, conservative,* and *benign,* taken from the article, are isolated below. Imagine for a moment that you feel a bit unsure about the conceptual meaning of these words. One of the first things to do is check the definitions in your dictionary.

Begin with the word *fatality.* What do you see immediately after the word? Your entry should be similar to the one below.

> **fa•tal** (fāt′l) *adj.* **1.** Causing or capable of causing death. **2.** Causing ruin or destruction; disastrous. **3.** Of decisive importance; fateful. **4.** Concerned with or determining destiny. **5.** *Obsolete.* Having been destined; fated. [ME, fateful < OFr. < Lat. *fātālis* < *fātum,* prophecy, doom. See FATE.]   ⑤
>
> ①   ② ③   ④
> **fa•tal•i•ty** (fā-tăl′ĭ-tē, fə-) *n., pl.* **-ties. 1.a.** A death resulting from an accident or a disaster. **b.** One killed in such an occurrence. **2.** The ability to cause death or disaster. **3.** The reality of being determined by fate. **4.** A decree made by fate; destiny. **5.** The quality of being doomed to disaster.

The information presented in parentheses (*1*) is the phonetic spelling of the word to aid pronunciation. If you are unsure of how to pronounce a word, this can be helpful. Remember, learning the meaning of a word without being able to pronounce it in your own conversations is somewhat useless. You learn words so you can use them in written and oral communication.

The second item of information typically found in a dictionary definition is the part of speech of the word (*2*). In the *fatality* entry, "*n*" stands for "noun."

Because some words can also be used as adjectives (adj), adverbs (adv), or verbs (v), it is important to scan the entire entry quickly for the part of speech that matches how the word is used in the context you are reading. If you forget what the abbreviations used in your dictionary mean, consult the key, usually located at the beginning or near the end of the book.

The third item of information given for *fatality* is another abbreviation (*3*). What does "*pl*" stand for? Check your key to see. Generally, the third piece of information in a dictionary entry provides the inflected forms, that is, how words can be changed to express different relationships within sentences. Hence, the word *fatality* can also occur as *fatalities*, a plural of the noun *fatality*.

Now you finally get to the definitions (*4*)! Here is a word of advice before you read the possibilities. Each dictionary has its own system or hierarchy for arranging definitions. Definitions in *The American Heritage College Dictionary* are listed analytically—that is, they are listed "according to central meaning clusters." Other dictionaries list definitions in order of historical usage, thus making their last definition the most current or widely used. Still others list the most current or widely used definition first. When using a dictionary, always check the policy for arrangement by reading the user's guide or introduction. If you are not using *The American Heritage College Dictionary*, check to see how your dictionary orders definitions.

Definition 1a for *fatality* is "a death resulting from an accident or a disaster." Does that fit the sentence from Reading A? Try it out.

The deaths resulting from disasters estimate was 21 times what the EPA had forecast earlier.

The definition appears to fit, makes sense in the paragraph, and communicates meaningful information. Check to see how many characteristics of strong definitions the entry for *fatality* has.

One other piece of information that is often included in dictionary entries is a summary of the word's etymology, or history. Note that for the word *fatality* no etymology is given. But if you look at the entry for the root word *fatal*, you will find the etymological information. We locate this information for you with the number *5*. Using etymological information is discussed later in this chapter.

The *fatality* entry is rather basic, so let's try another word that is a bit more difficult. Look up the word ***conservative*** in your dictionary and quickly scan the entire entry. It should be similar to the entry below.

con•ser•va•tive (kən-sûr′ve-tĭv) *adj.* **1.** Favoring traditional views and values; tending to oppose change. **2.** Traditional; restrained in style: *a conservative suit.* **3.** Moderate; cautious. **4.a.** Of or relating to the political philosophy of conservatism. **b.** Belonging to a conservative party, group, or movement. **5. Conservative.** Of or belonging to the Conservative Party or the Progressive Conservative Party. **6. Conservative.** Of or adhering to Conservative Judaism. **7.** Tending to conserve; preservative. — *n.* **1.** One favoring traditional views and values. **2.** A supporter of political conservatism. **3. Conservative.** A member or supporter of the Conservative Party. **4.** *Archaic.* A preservative agent or principle. — **con•ser′va•tive•ly** *adv.* **con•ser′va•tiveness** *n.*

Notice that this entry is longer and contains more definitions than does *fatality.* Notice, too, that *conservative* can be used as an adjective and a noun. The other distinguishing feature is that the word *conservative* can be a proper noun or a proper adjective and thus is sometimes capitalized. This meaning of *conservative* refers to a specific political party in the United Kingdom. The capitalized version does not apply in the context of this chapter's reading because we are discussing estimates of ozone loss in the atmosphere, not political parties. Consequently, we will focus only on the uncapitalized word. Remember that many words in dictionaries can define a specific people or group. Sometimes you will be looking for these definitions, but most of the time you will be searching for the meaning of the uncapitalized word.

How is the word *conservative* used in Reading A? Is it an adjective or a noun? As used there, *conservative* is an adjective. Now select the most appropriate definition. Carefully examine definitions 1, 2, and 3, noting the example in italics in 2: "*a conservative suit.*" In this dictionary, examples are often provided and are signaled as examples through the use of a colon followed by the example in italics. Now examine definition 3. Which definition is the most appropriate? Does "cautious" or "moderate" fit the sentence?

Were any of our estimates of ozone layer loss too cautious?

This definition seems appropriate for the word *conservative* in this context.

Understanding Etymological Information in a Typical Entry.   When you analyze the *etymology*, or history, of a word, you can often find information that is interesting and useful in helping you understand and remember new words encountered in reading. Etymological information usually occurs between square brackets: [ ]. In *The American Heritage College Dictionary*, it follows all the definitions for a given root word. For example, if you examine the entry for *fatal* on page 84, you will see brackets after the last definition. Some dictionaries, however, place this information at the beginning of the entry. Check your dictionary to find where the etymological information is presented.

Use the glossary of abbreviations in the front of the dictionary to interpret the symbols within the brackets and to determine where the word originated. Return to the *fatal* entry. Inside the brackets you see the following:

[ME, fateful < OFr. < Lat. *fātālis* < *fātum,* prophecy, doom. See FATE.]

In *The American Heritage College Dictionary,* the most recent known pre–Modern English stage is given first, with each earlier stage following in sequence. In the example above, Middle English (ME), Old French (OFr.), and Latin forms have the same basic definition as shown by both the "<" mark as well as the two Latin examples given—*fatalis* and *fatum.* You may already know one of the more common meanings of *fatal:* "causing or capable of causing death" as in a *fatal* automobile accident. One of the most important things to observe about etymological entries is that most words have origins in other languages and have been evolving for long periods of time.

Let's examine a dictionary entry and etymology for the word *benign.* Remember that the first step in determining meaning is to check the context to determine the word's part of speech and to see what information you can gather about the word. As used in Reading A, *benign* is an adjective. The dictionary entry reads as follows:

> **be•nign** (bǐ-nīn′) *adj.* **1.** Of a kind and gentle disposition. **2.** Showing gentleness and mildness. **3.** Tending to exert a beneficial influence; favorable. See Syns at **favorable. 4.** *Medic.* Of no danger to health; not recurrent or progressive; not malignant. [ME *benigne* < OFr. < Lat. *benignus.* See **genə-*.] — **be•nign′ly** *adv.*

The entry above has four definitions. The last definition refers to something "not malignant," such as a benign tumor. Since this definition pertains to diseases and the author of Reading A is describing chemicals that are not chlorine based, this definition can be eliminated. An examination of the three remaining definitions reveals that definition 3 seems most appropriate to this context—tending to exert a beneficial influence.

By checking the etymological entry, we can learn more about *benign.* The word originated from Middle English, Old French, and the Latin root *benignus.* Since *benignus* means "well or beneficial," there appears to be a relationship between definition 3 and the word's etymology. If you were to check your own dictionary for words such as *benefactor, beneficial,* and *benediction* you would discover that these words are cognates of *benign* since they too originate from *benignus.*

The final step is to substitute definition 3 to determine whether it makes sense. Does this make sense?

> Chemicals that have a beneficial influence can do the job of other solvents that contain chlorine.

Interpreting dictionary entries is a matter of understanding the format of your dictionary and taking the time to interpret the symbols and abbreviations used in the etymological entry. Your understanding of a new word can be enhanced by the interpretation of etymological entries. Some words have fascinating histories and etymological entries. Some of these histories are so intriguing that you will be able to place the word's meaning in your long-term memory and retrieve it forever. In the next section, we discuss some of these words and their entries.

Unusual Word Origins in Etymological Entries.   Although many of the more difficult English words do originate from languages no longer spoken, there are many other sources for English words besides Latin and Greek. A considerable number of words that we use daily originate from modern languages such as French, Spanish, and German. For example, the words *elite*, *naive*, and *gourmet* all come from French words and expressions.

Other words can trace their history to stories of interesting people and places. The word *maverick*, for instance, owes its beginnings to a man named Sam Maverick who was a Texas rancher in the 1800s. Mr. Maverick had such a soft heart that he refused to brand his cattle. Cattle rustlers called his unmarked cattle *mavericks*. The label has been applied to people who are independent or rebellious because they do not follow the crowd or general trends. When you check the etymology of *maverick* you will see that Samuel Maverick is listed as the source of the word.

When you read an etymological entry, make sure you look for the following sources of a word:

1. **Places**—Examples: *marathon, meander*
2. **Mythology**—Examples: *mentor, lunatic*
3. **Acronyms,** or the abbreviation of a series of words by using the first letters—Example: *laser* stands for <u>L</u>ight <u>A</u>mplification by <u>S</u>imulated <u>E</u>mission of <u>R</u>adiation
4. **Inventions**—Examples: *modem, boom box*
5. **Clips,** or the shortening of a word—Example: *fax* as a clip of *facsimile* or *perks* as a clip of *perquisites*
6. **Blends,** or the blends of sounds and meanings of two words—Examples: *Medicaid* is a blend of *medic(al)* and *aid; telecast* is a blend of *tele(vision)* and *(broad)cast*
7. **Names of people**—Examples: *maverick, gerrymander*
8. **Foreign languages**—Examples: *gourmet, cigar*

Depending on your dictionary, these other sources for a word's origin may be noted in the etymological information with brackets. If your dictionary does not fully explain the stories behind the words and you are interested in this, consider the following books as sources:

1. *Word Origins and Their Romantic Stories* by Wilfred Funk (New York: Funk and Wagnalls, 1950)
2. *Name into Word* by Eric Partridge (London: Secker and Warburg, 1949)
3. *Hog on Ice* by Charles Funk (New York: Paperback Library, 1973)
4. *Words from the Myths* by Isaac Asimov (Boston: Houghton Mifflin Company, 1961)
5. *Origins: A Short Etymological Dictionary of Modern English* by Eric Partridge (New York: Macmillan, 1962)
6. *The Oxford English Dictionary, Second Edition*, by J. A. Simpson and Edmund S. Weiner (Oxford: Oxford University Press, 1989)

Connotation: Links to Experience

Now that you have a good idea about denotative, or dictionary, word knowledge, let's examine *connotation*—a more abstract part of word knowledge that also leads to conceptual understanding. Connotation refers to the knowledge about words gained from experiences.

It should be apparent by now that a dictionary alone rarely provides conceptual knowledge. Stage 4 word knowledge generally comes from extensive reading and numerous encounters with words used in different contexts. Evidence for this claim stems from what is known in the study of words as the *Sapir-Whorf Hypothesis*. Simply, this hypothesis states that you can think only about ideas that your language system can explain or understand. For example, if you are from a state with a tropical climate, such as Florida or some portions of California, you see palm trees daily. People who live in these areas don't see just palm trees; they see many different kinds of palms—coconut palms, date palms, royal palms, fishtail palms, and the like. Individuals who visit these climates generally see only "palm trees" and do not differentiate among palms because the specific kinds are not part of their language system. This sort of differentiation helps develop your connotative knowledge about words. As previously stated, what you read in a dictionary provides denotative knowledge; what you add to the knowledge of words through your own experiences are the connotative elements. In order for you to know a word conceptually, both elements must be present.

To illustrate the difference between denotation and connotation, we'll start with an easy example. If you look up *dog* in *The American Heritage College Dictionary*, the entry reads as follows:

> **dog** (dôg, dǒg) *n.* **1.** A domesticated canid (*Canis familiaris*) related to foxes and wolves and raised in many breeds. **2.** Any of various members of the family Canidae, such as the dingo. **3.** A male animal of the family Canidae, esp. of the domesticated breed. **4.** Any of various other animals; the prairie dog. **5.** *Informal.* **a.** A person: *you lucky*

dog! **b.** A contemptible person: *You stole my watch, you dog.* **6.** *Slang.* **a.** An unattractive or uninteresting person; **b.** An inferior product or creation. **7. dogs.** *Slang.* The feet. **8. andiron. 9.** *Slang.* A hot dog; a wiener. **10.** Any hooked or U-shaped metallic devices used for gripping or holding heavy objects. **11.** *Astron.* A sun dog. — *adv.* Totally; completely. Often used in combination: *dog-tired.* — *tr.v.* **dogged, dog•ging, dogs. 1.** To track or trail persistently. **2.** To hold or fasten with a dog. — *idioms.* **dog it.** *Slang.* To fail to expend the effort to accomplish something. **go to the dogs.** To go to ruin; degenerate. **put on the dog.** *Informal.* To make an ostentatious display. [ME *dogge* < OE *docga*.]

If someone had told you as a young child to look up the meaning of the word *dog* because you were expected to learn what *dog* means from a dictionary, you probably would have had little idea what a dog is after seeing this definition. In fact, if someone gave you that definition without telling you that it is the definition of *dog*, you might assume that it is describing a cat or some other animal.

How could you define *dog* so that a reader would be sure of what you were talking about? Would it be possible to construct an effective definition of *dog* that meets all five of the criteria mentioned earlier in this chapter? For this example, it probably is not particularly important to have an effective definition because most people have had a variety of experiences with dogs. Unless you have been isolated, you not only can distinguish a dog from a cat, but you also can distinguish among different breeds of dogs. If your brother calls and tells you that he just bought a Great Dane puppy, you will have a much different mental picture than if he tells you that he just bought a poodle. Your knowledge of dogs has resulted not from any dictionary but from the variety of experiences you have had.

Other connotations that you might have about dogs probably occur as a result of your experiences. If you grew up with dogs, always had one or more dogs as pets, and your dogs slept in your bed or shared cookies with you, your reaction when you see a dog, or even when you hear the word, will be a positive one. However, if you never had a dog because your mother thought they were nasty, dirty creatures with fleas, or if you were bitten by a dog, your reaction when you see a dog or hear the word might be one of disgust or fear. These elements of words cannot be written in a dictionary. Rather, we learn these connotations through everyday experiences—reading widely, interactions with others, and the media.

A second example will illustrate the role that connotation plays in a more realistic reading situation. You encounter the following sentence during reading:

The senator's *gaffe* caused the audience to laugh out loud, but the senator continued his speech without pause.

Context does not provide much information. *Gaffe* could be a joke or some sort of action. You really can't tell what. When you look up the word you find the following definition:

gaffe also **gaff** (găf) *n.* **1.** A clumsy social error. **2.** A blatant mistake or misjudgment. [Fr. < OFr., hook. See GAFF[1].]

If you reread the characteristics of a good definition, you will find that the definition for *gaffe* is ineffective. Just what is "a clumsy social error"? And *blatant* in the second definition may be another unfamiliar word. Asked to generate a sentence for *gaffe*, having never seen the word before, you would face a difficult task. You might write something like "My friend made a *gaffe* when he dripped strawberry sauce all over his shirt in the expensive French restaurant." Neither dictionary nor context gives you any information about which "social errors" constitute *gaffes* and which do not.

If you possessed more connotative knowledge of *gaffe*, however, you might know that a *gaffe*, as indicated in the original context, is usually something spoken and is generally a mistake that an individual does not realize he or she has committed. Understanding such connotative elements suggests that although dripping strawberry sauce on your shirt may not be considered socially acceptable, it would also not be considered a *gaffe*. Therefore, the connotative elements of a word, though not revealed in a dictionary, are as important as a dictionary's denotative entries.

Using Context and a Dictionary

As mentioned earlier, words by themselves have no meaning; only when they are put into some context is meaning effectively communicated. This is why it is crucial to know how a word is used before you look it up in a dictionary. There are three key situations in which it is particularly crucial to use both context and a dictionary:

1. When words can be used as more than one part of speech
2. When the word is used as only one part of speech but can take on either slightly or dramatically different meanings
3. When you are dealing with content-specific terms

Words as Different Parts of Speech.   Many words can be used as different parts of speech. Sometimes the part of speech changes the meaning of the word only slightly, but on other occasions, meanings change dramatically.

There are several examples of such words in "A Bigger Hole in the Ozone." As an example, let's look at the word ***anchors,*** which is found in the following context:

> Ultraviolet radiation can also cause cataracts, weaken the immune system, damage crops and disrupt the reproduction of plankton that ***anchors*** the marine food chain.

Although you might be familiar with one of the noun forms of *anchor*, in this context, *anchor* is used as a verb. When you look up the word in the dictionary, you find the following entry:

> an•chor (ăng′kər) *n.* **1.** *Naut.* A heavy object attached to a vessel and lowered overboard to keep the vessel in place either by its weight or by its flukes, which grip the bottom. **2.** A rigid point of support, as for securing a rope. **3.** A source of security or stability. **4.** *Sports.* **a.** An athlete who performs the last stage of a competition. **b.** The end of a tug-of-war team. **5.** An anchorperson. — *v.* **-chored, -chor•ing, -chors.** — *tr.* **1.** To hold fast by or as if by an anchor. **2.** *Sports.* To serve as anchor for (a team or competition). **3.** To narrate or coordinate (a newscast). — *intr. Naut.* To drop anchor or lie at anchor. [ME *anker, ancher* < OE *ancor* < Lat. *ancora, anchora* < Gk. *ankura*.]

In this situation, even with several verb definitions given, it still is not totally apparent which one is best, so it's important to think through the three transitive verb definitions. The third, "to narrate or coordinate," fails to fit this context. The context states that plankton *anchors* the food chain, but here it does not mean that plankton coordinates the food chain. Similarly, the second definition, "to serve as anchor for," does not fit, especially given the two sample phrases.

There is only one choice left. *Anchor* in this context must have something to do with holding fast or fixing, as suggested in the first definition. If you think of someone or something that secures or fixes as making something firm or stable, then, yes, plankton can hold fast or fix. What the author of Reading A is trying to communicate by using *anchor* in this context is that plankton makes the food chain stable. Without plankton, the food chain would not function as nature intended.

Words That Have Changed Meaning.   In addition to making sure that you know what part of speech a word is used as, there is a second reason why using context in combination with a dictionary becomes important. Sometimes the part of speech remains the same, but the meaning changes—sometimes dramatically, at other times only slightly. An example of a dramatic change comes to mind with the term *CD.* Out of context, how do you know what kind of *CD* we are referring to? Is it the music kind—the abbreviation that comes from *compact disc*—or is it a *certificate of deposit* that you might purchase as a way of saving money for the future?

Another example is the word *cookie* found in Reading B, "Getting Personal," in Chapter 1. Everyone could select the traditional definition of *cookie* from the dictionary—"a small, usually flat crisp cake made from sweetened dough." Almost everyone also has connotative meanings attached to the word *cookie* as well. You might remember helping your mother bake cookies during the holidays or having your favorite kind of cookie when you came home from school. But look on page 20 to see how the word *cookie* can be used in another context. That use of the word is so new that it probably isn't in most dictionaries yet. There *cookies* are "tiny coded identifiers deposited on your computer's hard drive through your browser." If you use the Internet, and particularly if you make purchases over the Internet, you probably have *cookies* on your hard drive—messages designed especially for you. For example, the authors of this text use the Internet to seek out hotels, restaurants, and airline tickets, and both of us have on our hard drives *cookies* that advertise these services. Now you can not only eat a cookie but also have one on your computer too!

A similar, though certainly not as dramatic, example occurs with the word **regulators** from "A Bigger Hole in the Ozone." It reads:

> Eliminating CFCs before 2000, though, would not make much difference, because so many of the chemicals are already on their way to the stratosphere. In effect, **regulators** are running out of ideas.

The American Heritage College Dictionary indicates two major different definitions of **regulator**, a noun:

> **reg•u•la•tor** (rĕg′yə-lā′tər) *n.* **1.** One that regulates, as: **a.** The mechanism in a watch by which its speed is governed. **b.** A clock used as a standard for timing other clocks. **c.** A device used to maintain uniform speed in a machine; a governor. **d.** A device used to control the flow of gases, liquids, or electric current. **2.** One that ensures compliance with laws and regulations.

In this instance, the correct definition is relatively easy to select, since in context it is obvious that the **regulator** in question is a person, not some device. The only definition that could refer to a person is the second one. But "one that ensures compliance with regulations" tells us little. At this point you would look up the words *ensure*, *compliance*, and *regulations* to determine that the definition means "one who makes sure that others obey rules or laws." Now you are ready to put the two pieces of information together to conclude that the **regulators** are individuals who direct how much and what kind of CFCs are allowed to be released into the stratosphere.

Content-Specific Terms.   Perhaps the most important situation in which to use context as well as a dictionary is when you encounter difficult content-specific terms. Content-specific terms are words unique to a specialized field or course of study. You have encountered content-specific words already in this text, and you will encounter them in courses such as psychology, sociology, and biology. These words often appear on exams. Consequently, you will need an organized approach to determine their meaning. As discussed in Chapter 2, several generative strategies can provide significant assistance in learning content-specific words. A dictionary may not be as helpful as some of these generative strategies, but it still can be used if certain modifications are made.

Let's examine these modifications with the word *stratosphere,* from "A Bigger Hole in the Ozone." The context reads as follows:

> Eliminating CFCs before 2000, though, would not make much difference, because so many of the chemicals are already on their way to the *stratosphere.*

As with general vocabulary words, the first step should be to check the surrounding words and sentences for definitional hints. In this situation, context does not provide much information. We do know that *stratosphere* is a noun in this sentence. Hence, the second step is to check a dictionary or a glossary for more information. Rather than using a general dictionary, it is usually better, if possible, to check a specialized dictionary for the meaning of content-specific words. Check your library's reference section for a listing of these specialized dictionaries, as there is one for almost every content area. Some of the most common ones are Taber's *Cyclopedic Medical Dictionary, Harvard Dictionary of Music, A Dictionary of Economics,* and *A Dictionary of Anthropology.* You should also check the back of your textbook, because many textbooks have their own specialized glossaries.

To understand the difference between a glossary entry and a dictionary entry when you are looking at content-specific words, carefully read the following two entries, the first from a dictionary and the second from a textbook glossary:

> **strat•o•sphere** (străt′ə-sfîr′) *n.* **1.** The region of the atmosphere above the troposphere and below the mesosphere. **2.** An extremely high or the highest point or degree on a ranked scale. [Fr. *stratosphère* : Lat. *stătus*, a spreading out; see STRATUS + *-sphère*, sphere (< OFr. *espere*; see SPHERE).]

> **Stratosphere**—a region of the atmosphere between approximately 10 to 35 miles in altitude, where temperatures rise and weather is consistent; airplanes fly in this region.

The dictionary entry is confusing. The textbook glossary definition is superior and useful because it is precise and meaningful to someone who is not an environmental expert or science major.

The final step is to check the glossary definition to make sure it fits the original context. Does the following make sense?

Chemicals are on their way up to a region approximately 10 to 35 miles high in altitude.

In the *stratosphere* example, the glossary was more useful than the dictionary entry and surrounding words and sentences. In the next example, we will examine another content-specific word, *chlorofluorocarbons,* for which context is more helpful in determining the meaning. The word first appears in the following sentence:

In 1987, 24 nations meeting in Montreal pledged that, by the year 2000, they would halve their production of *chlorofluorocarbons* (CFCs), chemicals that destroy ozone.

Notice that an initial explanation of CFCs is provided in this sentence: CFCs are chemicals that destroy ozone. Obviously, this is a partial definition, but it is a start toward conceptual understanding of the word. The next step is to check a dictionary or a glossary for further details. You gain a bit more information from the dictionary entry below.

chlo•ro•fluor•o•car•bon (klôr′ō-flŏŏr′ō-kär′bən, -flôr′-, -flōr′-, klōr′-) *n.* Any of various halocarbon compounds consisting of carbon, hydrogen, chlorine, and fluorine, once used widely as aerosol propellants and refrigerants and now believed to cause depletion of the atmospheric ozone layer.

You now know that CFCs are compounds that contain carbon, hydrogen, chlorine, and fluorine, but an analysis of the word itself might have told you this. You also learn from the dictionary entry that CFCs were once widely used as refrigerants and in aerosol cans.

To add further to the information given in the dictionary definition and the initial sentence, you can check the rest of the article for additional explanations or characteristics of CFCs. By scanning the rest of Reading A, you learn the following information about CFCs:

1. They will be banned in the year 2000 by 90 countries. Hence, they seem to be dangerous.
2. CFCs stay in the atmosphere for decades. Therefore, they are potent and long-lasting.
3. The Environmental Protection Agency (EPA) is looking for substitutes for CFCs, but this task has been difficult. This is especially true for refrigerators and air conditioners.
4. Some scientists believe that eliminating CFCs would not make much difference, since so many CFCs are already in the stratosphere.

With this information from the article and the dictionary you should be able to write a precise and useful definition for **_chlorofluorocarbons_**. Take some time and write your definition below:

My definition for CFCs: _____

_____

_____

Your definition should be similar to this one: "CFCs are compounds of carbon, hydrogen, chlorine, and fluorine that appear to have longlasting and dangerous effects on the ozone layer since they can last in the atmosphere for decades. CFCs are used in refrigerators, air-conditioners, and aerosol propellants. Presently, 90 developed nations have agreed to ban CFCs by the year 2000, but other countries have yet to do likewise." This definition illustrates the detail necessary for conceptual understanding of a word and the precision necessary for success in content-area courses.

In this Building Blocks section you learned how to effectively use the dictionary to improve your conceptual understanding of words and how to evaluate dictionary definitions. Now you're ready to apply this new knowledge. Do the Figuring It Out, Practicing It, and Applying It activities for Readings A, B, and C. These activities will enable you to learn new words as well as to practice your new-found vocabulary skills.

Vocabulary Activities

 Figuring It Out

A.1 DIRECTIONS: Look up each of the 14 targeted words from "A Bigger Hole in the Ozone" in the dictionary. In the space provided, write a definition reflecting the way the word is used in context. Partial context has been provided for you, but as you work through this exercise, you should return to Reading A to review the full context.

1. ". . . save **_endangered_** species." _____

_____

2. "... would halve their production of *chlorofluorocarbons* (CFCs) ..."

   _____

3. "... the problem is far *graver* than anyone thought." _____

   _____

4. "The *fatality* estimate ..." _____

   _____

5. "... what the EPA had *forecast* earlier." _____

   _____

6. "... plankton that *anchors* the marine food chain." _____

   _____

7. "... raises the *incidence* of skin cancer ..." _____

   _____

8. "'... they are far too *conservative.*'" _____

   _____

9. "... EPA would *intensify* its efforts ..." _____

   _____

10. "... in finding *benign* chemicals ..." _____

    _____

11. "... do the job of chlorine-based *solvents* ..." _____

    _____

12. "... would *cripple* their economies." _____

    _____

13. "... already on their way to the *stratosphere*." _____

_____

14. "... *regulators* are running out of ideas." _____

_____

 Practicing It

A.2 DIRECTIONS: Read each sentence carefully. If the boldfaced word is used correctly, circle *C* and go on to the next item. If the boldfaced word is used incorrectly, circle *I* and then make the sentence correct.

C I   1. The Olympic athlete's chances for winning a medal were *crippled* when it was discovered that he had been taking steroids.

C I   2. After failing the accounting midterm, the business major decided to *intensify* her efforts by avoiding class and skipping the daily assignments.

C I   3. The television announcer *forecast* snow, but the weather turned warm and we had only rain.

C I   4. After learning that the damage to her car was *graver* than she expected, Louise felt a sense of relief and happiness.

C I   5. Chris was extremely depressed when the doctor told him that his tumor was *benign*.

C I   6. Many zoos and corporations are attempting to preserve *endangered* animals with special educational programs.

C I   7. In the United States, the *incidence* of measles and smallpox has significantly decreased.

C I   8. The bus driver, who had caused several passenger *fatalities*, was rewarded with a bonus and a letter of appreciation.

C I   9. When estimating how much pizza and how many beverages are needed for a party of hungry college students, it is always wise to be *conservative*.

C I   10. The chairperson of our club, an organized and dedicated worker, *anchors* the goals and projects we have established.

C   I   **11.** *Regulators* trained in airline safety turned out to investigate the procedures used by the pilots and flight attendants prior to the crash.

C   I   **12.** Anthony flew his kite through the *stratosphere.*

C   I   **13.** The United States and Britain are encouraging underdeveloped nations to use more *chlorofluorocarbons.*

C   I   **14.** Martin used the *solvent* to strip paint from the cupboards.

 Applying It

A.3   DIRECTIONS: Answer the following questions, being as specific as possible in order to demonstrate your understanding of the boldfaced words.

1. What have 90 countries agreed to do to help reduce the problem of *chlorofluorocarbons?*

_____

2. Give some examples to illustrate that the ozone problem is *graver* than most people ever imagined.

_____

3. What is the estimated *fatality* count for people dying from skin cancer in the United States? How does this *forecast* differ from the one provided earlier by the EPA?

_____

4. Why would abandoning CFCs *cripple* the economies of some countries?

_____

5. How has the EPA *intensified* its efforts to find solutions to the problems affecting the ozone layer?

_____

6. Are *regulators* opimistic in their attempts to find a solution? Why or why not?

_____

READING B

Reading B, entitled "'You Could Get Raped,'" presents a true story about a young woman who was stalked by someone over the Internet. Pay particular attention to how the targeted words are used in context so that you can select the most accurate dictionary definitions. You also might want to think about the pros and cons of going online. Before reading the article and completing the Vocabulary Activities, evaluate your present understanding of each of the 23 targeted words. Circle 1, 2, or 3 to indicate how familiar you are with each word (see page 4 for an explanation of the rating system).

Level of Understanding

alleged	1	2	3
anonymity	1	2	3
arraignment	1	2	3
compelled	1	2	3
devastating	1	2	3
doggedly	1	2	3
doting	1	2	3
encrypted	1	2	3
hysterical	1	2	3
M.O.	1	2	3
modest	1	2	3
ominous	1	2	3
placid	1	2	3
rebuffed	1	2	3
salacious	1	2	3
skittish	1	2	3
solicitations	1	2	3
spawned	1	2	3
undeterred	1	2	3
unwittingly	1	2	3

verify	1	2	3
vixen	1	2	3
wrenching	1	2	3

"You Could Get Raped"   *by Donna Foote and Sarah Van Boven*

The inside story of one young woman's terrifying ordeal at the hands of a cyberstalker.

Randi Barber had never heard anything as frightening as the messages on her answering machine. The 28-year-old North Hollywood, Calif., woman started getting the calls in early 1998: dirty **solicitations** from several different men. But one April day, Barber learned just how scared she could be when a stranger knocked on her apartment door. He left after she hid silently for a few minutes, but phoned her apartment later. "What do you want?" she pleaded. "Why are you doing this?" Puzzled by the **hysterical** note in her voice, the man explained that he was responding to the sexy ad she had placed on the Internet.

"What ad? What did it say?" Barber asked. "Am I in big trouble?"

"Let me put it to you this way," the caller said. "You could get raped."

Barber didn't own a computer and had never been on the Web, but it didn't take her long to figure out that she was at the center of a nightmarish criminal plot. Over the next few months, Barber would discover that a stalker had assumed her identity in cyberspace and was posting ads on the Internet seeking men to fulfill kinky sexual desires. But the content of the messages wasn't the most disturbing part. The mysterious stalker was giving out Barber's address, directions to her home, details of her social plans and even advice on how to short-circuit her alarm system.

He was also **unwittingly** leaving **encrypted** clues. Last November, after an investigation by the FBI, the Los Angeles district attorney and the L.A. County Sheriff's Department, police arrested an acquaintance of Barber's named Gary Dellapenta under a California law that criminalizes stalking and harassment on the Internet; the 50-year-old security guard pleaded not guilty to that charge, computer fraud and solicitation for rape at a preliminary hearing in January, and his **arraignment** is scheduled for this week. Even veteran cops who have seen cybercrime explode in recent years are stunned by this case. "The Internet is presenting us with criminal-justice issues we haven't seen before," says one law-enforcement official.

"This person was sitting in his house before a computer screen moving would-be rapists around like chess pieces. It's one of the scariest things you can imagine."

Randi Barber can attest to that. A religious woman who grew up the only child of **doting** parents in the **placid** northern suburbs of Los Angeles County, Barber was unprepared for the **wrenching** toll the stalking has taken on her life. "You don't realize how valuable your privacy is till someone takes it away," she told *Newsweek* in an exclusive interview. "I feel dirty—even though I haven't even been touched. At work, I felt embarrassed to look people in the face. You can't believe what's happening to you." Before Dellapenta was taken into custody, Barber sometimes left her job at an Encino real-estate firm and slept in her car rather than return to her empty apartment. And even with her **alleged** stalker in jail, she is still so depressed that she feels physically sick.

But while Barber describes herself as "a **skittish** person," the investigators who eventually worked with her say a better description is "gutsy." Within days of receiving the first batch of **ominous** phone calls, she went to the police and filed a report. And when they told her they couldn't help, she **doggedly** started working the case herself. "I couldn't just sit there and let this happen to me," Barber remembers. "I had to know who he was." She didn't change her phone number, and she didn't panic. Barber kept the taped phone messages—as awful as they were—and called each creep back to explain that she was a victim, not a **vixen.** Two men cooperated with her request for help in tracing the culprit, and one sent her hard copies of some of his X-rated e-mails. In the meantime, Tom Barber, Randi's father, got online. "I knew I had to some way or another identify him and stop him," he says. "So I became a computer expert. I began to spend hours on the Internet." Within a week, he found the ads.

By August, Randi and her father had plenty of evidence—and a prime suspect in mind. Barber hadn't forgotten the unwanted advances she'd parried from Gary Dellapenta during 1996. She had met the security guard through a friend, but the twice-divorced Dellapenta (who lives in a **modest** stucco bungalow with his 80-year-old mother) made her uncomfortable. When he started making overtures, she **rebuffed** him. **Undeterred,** he sent flowers and a small gift, continued to call and even joined her church. After church elders intervened, the unwanted advances ceased. But months later the phone calls began.

The authorities started working in earnest on Barber's case once Randi and her father handed over the e-mails—and Dellapenta's name. At that point, says Tom Barber, "the mouse became the cat." FBI agent Mark Wilson and D.A. investigator Brian Hale traced the e-mails from the Web sites at which they were posted to the servers used to access the sites. Search warrants **compelled** the Internet companies to identify the user. All the paths led police back to Dellapenta. "When you go on the Internet, you leave fingerprints—we can tell exactly where you've been," says sheriff's investigator Mike Gurzi, who would eventually **verify** that all the e-mails originated from Dellapenta's computer after studying his hard drive. The alleged stalker's **M.O.** was tellingly simple: police say he opened up a number of free Internet e-mail accounts pretending to be Barber, posted the crude ads under a **salacious** log-on name and started e-mailing the men who responded. Dellapenta was arrested in November; his attorney is not commenting publicly on the case.

Even now, Barber knows very little about her alleged cyberstalker. Dellapenta's court records show he and his second wife filed for divorce in January 1996—just about the time Randi's harassment began—and has no prior criminal record. What he did seem to have was an extraordinary amount of anger. According to testimony given by the FBI's Wilson at the preliminary hearing, Dellapenta admitted that he had "inner rage" directed at Barber, and that he was seeing a psychologist because he "could not stop himself" from sending smutty e-mail. "This is not over when it's over," says Barber, her dark brown eyes filled with fear. The illusion of **anonymity** on the Internet has **spawned** a new generation of criminals who do things behind the cover of a computer screen they might otherwise never even consider. And as Randi Barber knows, the consequences can be **devastating.** ∎

Comprehension Quick-Check

After reading "'You Could Get Raped,'" ask your instructor for a copy of the Comprehension Quick-Check Quiz.

Vocabulary Activities

 Figuring It Out

B.1 DIRECTIONS: Look up each boldfaced word in your dictionary; then circle the correct definition of each one. You may want to write the full definition on vocabulary cards, as outlined in Chapter 2. Before you make your selection, be sure to return to Reading B and see how the word is used in context.

1. "... her **alleged** stalker ..."
   a. unproven
   b. initial
   c. accused
   d. subsequent

2. "The illusion of **anonymity** on the Internet ..."
   a. safeness
   b. freedom
   c. not being known
   d. understanding

3. "... his *arraignment* is scheduled ..."
   a. trial
   b. training
   c. testimony
   d. court appearance

4. "Search warrants *compelled* the Internet companies ..."
   a. forced
   b. convinced
   c. suggested
   d. instructed

5. "... the consequences can be *devastating*."
   a. comforting
   b. long-term
   c. unpredictable
   d. overwhelming

6. "... she *doggedly* started working the case herself."
   a. clumsily
   b. wholeheartedly
   c. incidentally
   d. accidentally

7. "... the only child of *doting* parents ..."
   a. working
   b. responsible
   c. excessively loving
   d. divorced

8. "... leaving *encrypted* clues ..."
   a. apparent
   b. unretrievable
   c. odd
   d. scrambled code

9. "Puzzled by the *hysterical* note in her voice ..."
   a. calming
   b. loud
   c. extremely funny
   d. emotional

10. "The alleged stalker's *M.O.* was tellingly simple . . ."
    a. consistent way of doing something
    b. plan
    c. e-mail address
    d. mail order

11. ". . . who lives in a *modest* stucco bungalow . . ."
    a. expensive
    b. large
    c. shy
    d. not showy

12. ". . . the first batch of *ominous* phone calls . . ."
    a. unwelcomed
    b. threatening
    c. suggestive
    d. consistent

13. ". . . in the *placid* northern suburbs of Los Angeles County . . ."
    a. crowded
    b. noisy
    c. calm
    d. rural

14. ". . . she *rebuffed* him."
    a. encouraged
    b. betrayed
    c. dated
    d. rejected

15. ". . . posted the crude ads under a *salacious* log-on name . . ."
    a. fake
    b. belonging to another person
    c. sexually arousing
    d. disrespectful

16. ". . . describes herself as 'a *skittish* person' . . ."
    a. sensible
    b. nervous
    c. scared
    d. organized

17. "... dirty *solicitations* from several different men."
    a. offers
    b. magazines
    c. complaints
    d. words

18. "... has *spawned* a new generation of criminals ..."
    a. produced
    b. endangered
    c. prosecuted
    d. arrested

19. "*Undeterred*, he sent her flowers ..."
    a. doubtful
    b. not discouraged
    c. after the fact
    d. not planned

20. "He was also *unwittingly* leaving encrypted clues."
    a. understandably
    b. suggestively
    c. foolishly
    d. without knowledge of

21. "... who would eventually *verify* that all the e-mails ..."
    a. verbalize
    b. prove
    c. disclose
    d. deny

22. "... she was a victim, not a *vixen*."
    a. a woman who is honest
    b. a woman who lies
    c. a woman who is assertive or aggressive
    d. a woman who is hateful or spiteful

23. "... was unprepared for the *wrenching* toll ..."
    a. distressing
    b. long-term
    c. cautionary
    d. monetary

Practicing It

B.2 DIRECTIONS: Read each sentence carefully. If the boldfaced word is used correctly, circle *C* and go on to the next item. If the boldfaced word is used incorrectly, circle *I* and then make the sentence correct.

C I **1.** When Elaine became ***hysterical,*** her best friend urged her to calm down and to take some deep breaths.

C I **2.** The lake was so ***placid*** that it would have been unsafe to take the boat out to waterski.

C I **3.** Her ***modest*** income enabled her to have a beach house, drive a Porsche, and take yearly trips to Europe.

C I **4.** Kareem ***doggedly*** tried to solve the puzzle by looking up the answer in the back of his book after five minutes of effort.

C I **5.** Avery felt a ***wrenching*** feeling in his stomach when his wife said that she was divorcing him.

C I **6.** The dog that the Carters got at the Humane Society was terribly ***skittish*** because its previous owner had given him an abundance of love.

C I **7.** The ***ominous*** clouds warned us that bad weather was on the way.

C I **8.** The ***alleged*** bank robber was brought to court for his ***arraignment.***

C I **9.** Mason's ***salacious*** comments about other women ***spawned*** loving feelings in his new girlfriend.

C I **10.** The ***anonymity*** of Internet chat rooms ***compels*** some individuals to say things they normally wouldn't say.

C I **11.** ***Undeterred*** by a foot of snow, Jake decided to stay in bed rather than get up and go to class.

C I **12.** In a hurry, Lara ***unwittingly*** locked herself out of the house.

C I **13.** ***Doting*** parents often have a need to ***verify*** the exact whereabouts of their teenagers every minute of the day.

C I **14.** Marissa had the reputation of being quite the ***vixen*** because of her shy and quiet ways.

C I   **15.** When surfing the Web, it is easy to ignore the *solicitations* that seem to appear on every site.

C I   **16.** The *devastating* hurricane left little damage.

C I   **17.** The murderer's *M.O.* was to leave an *encrypted* message to make it easy to find him.

 Applying It

B.3 DIRECTIONS: For each of the following items, give an example that demonstrates your understanding of the boldfaced word.

1. A situation in which you have been *rebuffed* _____

_____

2. A *placid* scene _____

_____

3. Something that is done at an *arraignment* _____

_____

4. An *encrypted* message _____

_____

5. Something that might cause you to become *hysterical* _____

_____

6. A time when it would be important to *verify* dates _____

_____

7. A time when you might be *compelled* to work on something *doggedly* ____

_____

8. Something a *doting* parent might say _____

_____

9. Something that might be *devastating* to your garden _____

_____

10. A *wrenching* decision _____

_____

B . 4 D I R E C T I O N S : Answer the following questions, making sure to provide enough detail to demonstrate your understanding of the boldfaced words.

11. Why might someone who is getting ready to rob a bank act *skittish*? _____

_____

12. What kind of comment might *spawn* a *salacious* action? _____

_____

13. When might you want to do something *anonymously*? _____

_____

14. What might happen to you if you *allegedly* committed fraud? _____

_____

15. What kind of *solicitations* would be viewed as appropriate? _____

_____

16. Why might you be *undeterred* by *ominous* weather? _____

_____

17. What movie actress is considered by many to be a *vixen*? _____

_____

18. In your opinion, what is a ***modest*** income? _____

_____

19. What is meant when we say that serial killers have an ***M.O.***? _____

_____

20. What might happen if you ***unwittingly*** lost your wallet? _____

_____

READING C

Reading C, entitled "MLK: The Man and the Myth," focuses on little-known facts about Martin Luther King, Jr., and his nonviolent approach to civil rights. Think about what you already know about Martin Luther King, Jr., and then see how the information presented here fits with what you already know. Does any information in the article surprise you? As you read, pay particular attention to how the words are used in context so that you can select the most accurate dictionary definition. Before reading the article and completing the Vocabulary Activities, evaluate your present understanding of each of the 18 targeted words. Circle 1, 2, or 3 to indicate how familiar you are with each word (see page 4 for an explanation of the rating system).

Level of Understanding

denunciations	1	2	3
diverting	1	2	3
extol	1	2	3
galvanized	1	2	3
impasse	1	2	3
inundate	1	2	3
moribund	1	2	3
purveyor	1	2	3
rabid	1	2	3
redemptive	1	2	3
sanitized	1	2	3

scurrilous	1	2	3
siege	1	2	3
stigmatize	1	2	3
subversive	1	2	3
transfixed	1	2	3
turbulent	1	2	3
vortex	1	2	3

MLK: The Man and the Myth
by Jerry McKnight

Romanticizing of heroes does nation a disservice.

As the nation celebrates the birthday of Dr. Martin Luther King, Jr., we must not get caught up in a Let-Us-Now-Praise-Famous-Men mood that obscures the full meaning and tragedy of his life.

As in past years, today we **extoll** the Dr. King of the "We Shall Overcome" and "I Have a Dream" phase of the civil rights struggle, when black demands for social justice could no longer be deferred.

We will be **transfixed** all over again by the chilling images of Dr. King and the Southern Christian Leadership Conference (SCLC) as they stood up to police dogs and fire hoses with nonviolence and **redemptive** soul-force. From these struggles were born the Civil Rights Act of 1964 and the Voting Rights Act of 1965.

Dr. King emerged as a national celebrity, gathering honorary degrees, *Time*'s "Man of the Year" award, a papal audience and the 1964 Nobel Peace Prize.

But the hard reality was that by the end of 1965 the movement was at an **impasse,** unable to progress in the face of institutional racism in the North and the government's preoccupation with Vietnam. Dr. King became painfully aware that legislative and judicial victories did little to improve the lot of millions of blacks living in Northern ghettoes.

Hoping to extend their influences, the SCLC targeted then-Mayor Richard Daley's Chicago. But SCLC tactics of marching and praying did not overcome in Boss Daley's Chicago. After months of effort, King's "war on the slums" ended in bitter and bewildering defeat. His message of nonviolence to Northern black youth

"MLK: The Man and the Myth," by Jerry McKnight, in *Atlanta Journal and Constitution*, Jan. 15, 1990, p. A11. Reprinted by permission.

fell on deaf ears. Increasingly, he was either ignored or mocked by more militants as an "Uncle Tom."

On April 4, 1967, in an address at the Riverside Church in New York City, Dr. King finally broke his silence on Vietnam. In harsh language he accused the government of **diverting** funds from the poverty program to fuel the Asian war and for cruelly manipulating black youth by "sending them 8,000 miles away to guaranteed liberties in Southeast Asia which they had not found in southwest Georgia or East Harlem." Dr. King blasted the Johnson administration as "the greatest **purveyor** of violence in the world today."

Reaction to Dr. King's anti-war declaration was swift and almost uniformly negative; most of the black community's elites distanced themselves from his **denunciations.**

By the summer of 1967, Dr. King was no longer the confident hero we choose to remember, but a physically exhausted and isolated man, confused about the future and profoundly depressed. He feared that the Black Power movement would be exploited by anti-civil rights elements to **stigmatize** the entire movement.

Dr. King, however, found the inner strength to go on. During the last year of his life he went through a radical transformation. He suspended his earlier conviction that white racism could be overcome by appealing to the nation's moral conscience with the positive force of Christian love.

By 1967, it was clear to Dr. King that America had no moral conscience and was dominated by racism at home and abroad. He came to believe that America needed a revolution in values, ignited by a radical redistribution of economic and political power.

To begin shaking the power structure, Dr. King and his SCLC staff threatened a new march on Washington for the spring of 1968. Phase One of the Poor People's Campaign began with recruitment of thousands of the nation's poor—black, white, Chicano and native Americans—to encamp in a shantytown near the Capitol. In Phase Two, the poor-people's army, its ranks swollen by hundreds of thousands of allies from the peace movement and the Washington ghettoes, would engage in massive, non-violent civil disobedience. Protestors determined to peacefully dislocate the functioning of government would **inundate** Congress, the Labor Department and the Pentagon.

Dr. King felt these shock tactics were necessary to arouse a "**moribund,** insensitive Congress to life" and to grant the nation's poor an "Economic Bill of Rights" guaranteeing jobs, decent housing and a minimum income to those too young, too old or too disabled to work. The **siege** of Washington would not be lifted until these demands were met or all protesters jailed.

The shift of the civil rights movement away from racial justice to economic and political matters only heightened the threat Dr. King posed to the reigning powers in government. No one in Washington had a more deep-seated and *rabid* fear of *"subversive"* influences undermining the status quo than FBI Director J. Edgar Hoover.

As early as the summer of 1963, Mr. Hoover viewed Dr. King as a threat to his way of life, his bureaucracy and his vision of a white, Christian, harmonious America. It was, however, the political King of the Poor People's Campaign and the anti-war movement that *galvanized* Mr. Hoover's FBI to unleash a no-holds-barred campaign to destroy the man the bureau considered America's most dangerous militant.

Although we may prefer *sanitized* history, we must face this sobering fact. The man whose birthday we celebrate as a national holiday was during his last 10 years the most watched and perhaps the most harassed citizen in U.S. history.

The FBI monitored Dr. King's movements through every intelligence-gathering technique imaginable. The FBI even drafted *scurilous* editorials against Dr. King and placed them in "cooperative" newspapers. The 402-page index to the FBI's King files indicates that they are more than 250,000 pages long.

While tragically cut short, Dr. King's life was a fully committed one. He hoped to be known as a drum major for justice and peace during a *turbulent* time. Caught up in the *vortex* of events, Dr. King looked for radical—but never violent—solutions to save the soul of the country.

Yet he was more than the voice of a beautiful dream. Martin Luther King Jr. was a complex political man whose legacy deserves not whitewashing, but the honor of honest remembrance. ■

Comprehension Quick-Check

After reading "MLK: The Man and the Myth," ask your instructor for a copy of the Comprehension Quick-Check Quiz.

Vocabulary Activities

 ## Figuring It Out

C.1 DIRECTIONS: Locate the correct definition for each of the 18 targeted words from "MLK: The Man and the Myth." Write the word in the blank across from the correct definition. Be sure to return to Reading C to review the context, because the definitions listed below are contextual definitions, not necessarily the definitions most frequently used.

Targeted Word	*Definition*
1. _____	vulgar, coarse, or abusive
2. _____	acts of speaking out or condemning something publicly
3. _____	motionless as a result of amazement or awe
4. _____	a situation that draws everything to its center
5. _____	to praise
6. _____	inactive, deathlike
7. _____	changing course or direction
8. _____	raging or uncontrollable
9. _____	to characterize as disgraceful
10. _____	someone who declares something, usually publicly
11. _____	aroused to action
12. _____	made more acceptable by the removal of unpleasant features
13. _____	a situation in which no progress can be made
14. _____	intending to undermine an established government
15. _____	a long period of time
16. _____	to overwhelm
17. _____	unruly or restless
18. _____	able to restore feelings of honor or worth

Practicing It

C.2 DIRECTIONS: Select from Reading C the targeted word that makes sense in each of the following sentences. After you complete each sentence, read it out loud to make sure that the word you selected really does make sense.

1. Although _____ comments were often made about the congressman's many affairs, no one had any hard evidence that they had actually occurred.

2. The sea was so _____ that the fishing boats had to quickly return to the dock to avoid the risk of overturning.

3. After the professor's boring lecture, the entire class had glazed-over eyes and appeared _____ .

4. Always the _____ of bad tidings, the evening newscaster rambled on about floods, murders, and carjackings.

5. It seems as though in today's society, we _____ wealth and possessions rather than honesty and hard work.

6. The toddler was _____ by reruns of *Teletubbies*.

7. Advertisers _____ you with junk mail urging you to buy their products.

8. By _____ the clerk's attention, one of the robbers was able to slip her hand into the cash drawer and remove a large sum of money.

9. Carla may be loud and sometimes insensitive, but she does have several _____ qualities: she visits the elderly, volunteers at the hospital, and cares for her ill father.

10. If you frequently make _____ statements about the government in large public forums, the FBI might decide to monitor your speeches.

11. Peace talks between the Israelis and the Palestinians are likely to hit a(n) _____ if neither party is willing to compromise.

12. When Samantha Worth was running for mayor, her campaign volunteers

    _____ her supporters to get out and vote for her.

13. During the _____ of the Branch Davidian complex in

    Waco, Texas, many people died or were injured.

14. The CEO's constant _____ led many of the firm's vice pres-

    idents to seek employment elsewhere.

15. During the Holocaust, Jews were _____(d) when they were

    forced to wear the Star of David on their clothing.

16. Cantrell is a(n) _____ competitor! He's always trying to run

    faster, jump higher, and be in better shape than any of his teammates.

17. At the _____ of movements such as the women's movement

    and the civil rights movement there is usually a strong and appealing leader.

18. Because Tamara's cats had an infection, she _____ their bed-

    ding every night.

Applying It

C.3 DIRECTIONS: Answer the following questions, making sure to
provide enough detail to demonstrate your understanding of the boldfaced
words. Be sure to answer both parts of each question.

1. Is it common practice to *extol* the virtue of *scurrilous* activities? Why or
   why not?

   _____

2. Would you want to *sanitize* a cage that had held a *rabid* dog? Why or
   why not?

   _____

3. Would *turbulent* weather *inundating* a Caribbean island be cause for alarm if you were vacationing there? Why or why not?

_____

4. Would a *purveyor* of *moribund* news be welcome at a birthday party? Why or why not?

_____

5. Could you *galvanize* support for your political campaign by *denouncing* your opponent? Why or why not?

_____

6. Would the police want to *divert* traffic if a rockslide caused an *impasse*? Why or why not?

_____

7. Could *subversive* comments made during a speech *stigmatize* you as a troublemaker? Why or why not?

_____

8. Could you be *transfixed* on the *vortex* of a hurricane? Why or why not?

_____

▶ **Extending**

DIRECTIONS: Using your dictionary, determine the origins of the following words. You may wish to do this activity in small groups.

1. What is the origin of the word *mentor*? Who has been your *mentor*? ___

_____

2. What is the origin of the word *narcissism*? Whom do you know who could be described as a *narcissist*? _____

_____

3. What is the origin of the words *faux pas*? What has been your most embarrassing *faux pas*? _____

_____

4. What is the origin of the word *meander*? When have you *meandered*?

_____

5. What is the origin of the word *malapropism*? Give an example of a *malapropism*. (*Hint*: see *malapropos*.) _____

_____

6. What is the origin of the word *chortle*? Would you be pleased if someone *chortled* at one of your jokes? Is this word a blend or a clip? _____

_____

7. What is the origin of the word *curio*? Have you ever received a *curio*? _____

_____

8. What is the origin of the word *quixotic*? _____

_____

9. What is the origin of the word *nemesis*? Identify one of your *nemeses*. _____

_____

10. What is the origin of the word *snafu*? _____

_____

DIRECTIONS: Earlier in this chapter, we brought to your attention the idea that new words are being coined daily, especially words related to the use of computers and the Internet. Examples of some of these words (found in Chapter 1) include *profiling*, *e-mail spam*, and *banner spaces*. Others, not found in Chapter 1, include *surfing*, *computer trolls*, *browser*, and *bulletin boards*. Definitions of these words as they relate to computers may not even be in the dictionary, but it's always a good idea to check. Look up each of these words in the most recent dictionary you can find. See if you can find an appropriate definition. If the dictionary provides an appropriate definition, circle *Y* and write the definition in the space provided. If the dictionary lacks an appropriate definition, circle *N* and ask your computer-knowledgeable friends for help. Based on what you find out, write a definition in the space provided. Share these definitions with your classmates.

11. *profiling*   Y   N

Definition: _____

_____

12. *e-mail spam*   Y   N

Definition: _____

_____

13. *banner spaces*   Y   N

Definition: _____

_____

14. *surfing*   Y   N

Definition: _____

_____

15. *computer trolls*   Y   N

Definition: _____

_____

16. *browser*   Y   N

Definition: _____

_____

17. *bulletin board*   Y   N

Definition: _____

_____

Evaluating

Review and test yourself on the 55 targeted words in this chapter. Then ask your instructor for the comprehensive exam on these words.

Summary

This chapter focuses on several aspects of using a dictionary. Although dictionary definitions are an important tool for vocabulary development, they must be used wisely. Because the quality of dictionary entries may vary, it is important to use a variety of sources to gain conceptual word knowledge. It also is important to know the information contained in a dictionary entry and how to interpret it. This chapter explains how to use the entry and how to find interesting and often helpful information about a word by focusing on the etymological material. In addition, the denotative meanings of words and how word connotations help the reader to know a word at the conceptual level are discussed. This chapter concludes by discussing how to combine dictionary use with context in order to maximize word understanding.

CHAPTER

4 Word Elements

The verb *precipitate* originated from the Latin prefix *pre*, meaning "before," and the root *caput*, "head." Visualize a person dashing headlong into something. Today one definition for *precipitate* is "to move rapidly, recklessly, or unexpectedly."

Many individuals believe that knowledge of word elements can significantly increase your vocabulary because you will be able to figure out unknown words by examining a prefix, suffix, or root. Consider the word *incredible*. If you know that the root *cred* means "belief" or "believe" and that the prefix *in* means "not," you can estimate that the word *incredible* means "not believable." In this instance, understanding the meanings of a root and a prefix would be an important step for independently determining the meaning of an unknown word. But learning word elements is not a cure-all. It is simply another piece of the puzzle, which, together with context and the dictionary, gives you one more option for understanding words in a generative fashion.

READING A

To put our discussion of roots, prefixes, and suffixes in a practical context, we present Reading A, a brief article entitled "The Pill That Transformed America." This selection focuses on research leading to the manufacture of the birth control pill. Before reading the article and completing the Vocabulary Activities, evaluate your present understanding of each of the 15 targeted words. Circle 1, 2, or 3 to indicate how familiar you are with each word (see page 4 for an explanation of the rating system).

Level of Understanding

anti-contraception	1	2	3
benefactor	1	2	3
biologist	1	2	3
complications	1	2	3
contraception	1	2	3
decade	1	2	3
depression	1	2	3
gynecologist	1	2	3
litigation	1	2	3
nonintrusive	1	2	3
ovulating	1	2	3
pharmaceutical	1	2	3
progesterone	1	2	3
prominent	1	2	3
spectacular	1	2	3

The Pill That Transformed America   *by Claudia Kalb*

From the day she opened her first clinic in 1916, Margaret Sanger longed for a simple, reliable, **nonintrusive** birth-control technique: a pill. Traditional "barrier" methods failed too often. They were overmatched by human error, mechanical failure and the ever-present factor of lust. Finally, in 1951 Sanger found a wealthy kindred spirit to fund her dream. She teamed up with Katherine McCormick, an MIT graduate whose father-in-law, Cyrus McCormick, had invented the mechanical reaper. Together they set out to help people prevent reaping what they were about to sow.

First, they needed a **biologist.** They found him in Gregory Pincus, head of the Worcester (Mass.) Foundation for Experimental Biology. Pincus was renowned for his breakthrough work fertilizing rabbit eggs in a test tube—and he was a man who reveled in meeting a challenge.

McCormick gave Pincus a $40,000 check. (She would be the pill's chief ***benefactor,*** contributing almost $2 million to the research.) Two strokes of good fortune followed quickly. First, chemists working separately in Mexico City and Chicago produced the pill's key ingredient, an oral form of ***progesterone.*** Back in 1928 the hormone, whose name comes from the Latin *pro* (in favor of) *gestare* (to bear), had been identified as central to sustaining pregnancy, and researchers thought it could be a critical ingredient in **contraception.** Later, scientists injected the hormone into rabbits: tricked into thinking they were pregnant, the animals stopped ***ovulating.*** But it wasn't until the early 1950s that chemists learned how to produce progesterone in a synthetic, oral form—just in time for Pincus.

His second lucky break came in 1952, when he bumped into the highly regarded Boston ***gynecologist*** Dr. John Rock, who was also studying progesterone. The two were an ideal match. Pincus had tested the hormone on animals, but not yet on women. Rock had the patients.

Massachusetts, where ***anti-contraception*** laws were among the staunchest in the nation, was an unlikely birthplace for the pill. Pincus and Rock, who was a ***prominent*** Roman Catholic, worked in secrecy. In 1954 Rock undertook the first clinical trial of Pincus's oral contraceptive on 50 volunteers with **spectacular** results: not a single ovulation. When larger trials were needed, the two moved their experiments out of the country—to Puerto Rico and Haiti. Both were successful.

The pill, from launch to FDA approval, took less than a ***decade***—a remarkable feat. It has plenty of critics, foremost among them the Catholic Church. Even feminists attacked it as a male creation with harmful side effects, including blood clots and ***depression;*** the ***complications*** have since been limited by fine-tuning hormonal dosages. In recent years, expensive ***litigation*** and other controversies have slowed investment in alternative methods. The pill remains in common use, and it's hard to think of a ***pharmaceutical*** that's had a greater effect on American life and mores. ■

Comprehension Quick-Check

After reading "The Pill That Transformed America," ask your instructor for a copy of the Comprehension Quick-Check Quiz.

Building Blocks—Roots, Prefixes, and Suffixes

When we use the term *word elements*, three words come to mind: *root, prefix,* and *suffix.* Before proceeding, it is important to have a clear understanding of each word element. We begin with a discussion of roots.

Roots

The most important word element is a word's *root*. The root is the word element from which most of the meaning is derived, and thus the root carries most of the denotative or dictionary meaning. Word elements cannot be broken down any further than a root and still carry meaning. However, two roots can be put together to form a word, such as the word *cinematography*, which is a combination of the roots *cinema* and *graph*.

Also, a root can be combined with either a prefix or a suffix, as in the case of *gynecologist* (the suffix *-ologist*, meaning "the study of," + the root *gyneco-*, meaning "women").

Some roots, such as *ego*, can stand alone. Others, called *combining roots*, must be combined with prefixes, other roots, or suffixes in order to communicate meaning. *Bio-*, *spec-*, and *cede-* are three examples of combining roots.

The following is a list of common roots, taken from Latin and Greek, that you will see in your reading. Keep in mind that this list, as well as the others that follow, is not all-inclusive. We include roots that are high-utility. How many of these common roots do you already know? Look over the list and the examples in the right-hand column.

Root	*Meaning*	*Example*
acer-, acr	sharp, bitter	acerbic, acrimony
amor-	love	amorous
arch-	chief, to rule	hierarchy
aud-	hear	audio (signal processor)
auto-	self	autocrat
bell(e)-	beautiful	embellishing
bio-	life	biosphere
cap-	take, hold	captivate
carn-	flesh	carnal
cede-	to go	preceded
cinema-	to move	cinematography
cogn-	to learn	cognitive
cosm-	universe, order	cosmopolitan
cred-	believe	credibility
dem-	people	demography
dict-	say, speak	dictated
ego-	I, self	egomania
fac-	make	facilitate
graph-	write	graphic simulator
gyneco-	woman	gynecologist
hier-	high	hierarchy
hydro-	water	dehydration

Root	Meaning	Example
idio-	one's own peculiar style	idiosyncrasies
jur-	to swear	conjures
man-, manu-	hand	manipulate, manual
mania-	madness	egomania
mis-, mit-	send	mission, emits
mort-	death	moribund
neur-	nerve	neurotic
ped-, pod-	foot	pedometer, podiatrist
photo-	light	photosensitive
phys-	nature	physiological
plac-, placa-	please	placate, complaisant
polis-	city, state	cosmopolitan
press-	to press	oppression
sen-	old	senile
sol-	alone	solace
son-	sound	sonority
spec-	to look, see	specter
sym-, syn-	same, together	sympathy, synthesis
vert-	turn	averted, convert
virtus-	goodness	virtuosity
viv-	live	vivacious
voc-	call	evocative

Prefixes

The next most important word elements are *prefixes*. Although prefixes do not add as much information as roots do, they bring more meaning than suffixes. Prefixes are those elements added to roots at the beginning of a word. Sometimes they can be removed from the root and what is left can stand on its own and make sense. Such is the case with the word *nonintrusive*. When the prefix *non-* is removed, what remains, *intrusive*, is a word that has meaning even without the prefix attached. If, however, the prefix *contra-* is removed from *contraception*, we are left with *-ception*, which makes no sense by itself. Another important quality of prefixes to note is that they change the meaning of the root word.

The following is a list of common prefixes. Look over the list and determine the ones you already know. Also, read the example word for each prefix.

Prefix	Meaning	Example
a-	from, down, away	aberration, abolition, acute
anti-	opposing, against	anti-establishment, anti-contraception
bi-	two	binary
com-, con-	with, together	components, consolation

Prefix	Meaning	Example
contra-	against, opposite	contraception
counter-	against	counterculture
de-	from, down	deterioration
di-	two	diatonic, dimension
dis-	not, apart	disintegrate, dispersed
e-, ec-	out	egress, eccentric
em-, en-	not, into, very	embodied, enhance
epi-	under	epicenter
equi-	just, equal, fair	equivalency
ex-	out, former	export, ex-president
hyper-	exceedingly	hyperactive
im-, in-	not	improper, inaccurate
il-, ir-	not	illogical, irrelevant
inter-	between	interactive
mal-	harmful	maladjusted
mis-	wrongly, badly	mistreat
non-	not	nonlove, nonintrusive
pro-	favoring, for	prolife, progesterone
pre-	before	pretest, precede
post-	after	postmodernism
pseudo-	false	pseudoscience
psych-	mind, mental	psychic
re-	back, again	reassemble, respondents
semi-	half	semiliterate
socio-	social, society	sociology
sub-	below, under	submerge
trans-	across	transition
un-	not, reversed	uncovered, unprecedented

Suffixes

The final word elements are *suffixes*. Suffixes carry the least amount of meaning. Their primary function is either to change the part of speech, as in *propose* to *proposition*, or to change the word to its plural form or to its past tense, as in the words *complications* and *spawned*. A few suffixes, such as *-logist*, which means "one who studies," extend the meaning of the root, as in the case of *biologist* and *gynecologist*, found in Reading A.

Read the list of common suffixes below. Notice that they have been divided by parts of speech.

Suffixes That Form Nouns	*Suffixes That Form Adjectives*
-ac	-able, -ible
-ance, -ancy	-ac, -ic
-dom	-al
-ence	-ant, -ent
-er, -or	-ary
-ess	-dom
-ion, -tion	-en
-ism	-ful
-ist	-ive
-ment	-like
-ness	-ous, -ious
-ology	-some
-ure	-y

Suffixes That Form Verbs	*Suffixes That Form Adverbs*
-ate	-ly
-ify	
-ize	

Advantages of Learning Word Elements

As mentioned above, learning a variety of word elements is not the only way to build your vocabulary. But when used along with other context and dictionary generative strategies, word elements can be helpful. Perhaps the biggest advantage in learning word elements is that learning one root can help you determine the meanings of more than one unfamiliar word. And while you may not be able to gain full conceptual knowledge of the word through knowing its root, when the root is combined with context, you probably will be able to determine a global meaning of the word. For example, an unabridged dictionary lists numerous words containing the root *bio-*, meaning "life." Thus, learning a root such as this becomes a real bargain. Knowing the meaning of *bio-* can help you determine the meanings of words such as *biosphere* and *biotechnology*, especially if you also use context. As mentioned in Chapter 3, these words are *cognates*, or related to each other.

Let's look at **benefactor**, an example from Reading A. The root **bene** means "well, good, or assisting." Let's combine that information with how the word is used in context. The sentence reads:

> McCormick gave Pincus a $40,000 check. (She would be the pill's chief **benefactor**, contributing almost $2 million to the research.)

By combining what we know about the meaning of this root with the context, we can speculate with a degree of certainty that a **benefactor** is someone who aids or supplies support, probably by contributing money. If we confirm our speculation by looking up the word in the dictionary, we find the following meaning:

benefactor—one that gives aid, esp. financial aid.

It is also interesting to note that there is a special word for a woman who gives aid, especially financial aid—*benefactress*. If you came across the word *benefactress* in your reading, would you be able to figure out what it means by already knowing that the suffix *-ess* means "female," as in *actress* or *lioness*? This is another example of how knowing the meaning of word elements can help you to determine the meaning of unknown words, especially when combined with other generative context and dictionary strategies.

Learning word elements has a tremendous payoff for students taking certain courses. You may not encounter many words with word elements in your history courses, but you will come across numerous words that use prefixes, roots, and suffixes in psychology and in the hard sciences, such as biology, chemistry, and physics. For example, imagine that your introductory psychology class is studying mental disorders. One group of disorders discussed is *phobias*. *Phobia* is a root word that can stand alone and make sense, or it can be combined with other roots, prefixes, or suffixes to form new words. *Phobia* means an intense and abnormal or unnatural fear. You probably know someone who is at least slightly *phobic*. If you are taking psychology, your textbook probably lists and defines a variety of phobias, each of which is a combination of either two roots or a prefix and a root.

For example, you might see the word *acrophobia*, meaning "fear of heights." The root *acro-* means "height" and of course the root *phobia* means "fear." Or you might see *pyrophobia*, "fear of fire." The root *pyro* means "fire." Do you know what fears people with the following phobias have: *herpetophobia*, *phonophobia*? How about *xenophobia*?

Using Word Elements in a Generative Manner

To use word elements as a generative strategy for vocabulary enrichment, remember two guidelines:

1. Try not to memorize the definitions of prefixes or roots in isolation. Attempting to learn definitions in this manner will often cause you to know a word at a superficial level rather than at a conceptual level.
2. If you guess about the meaning of a word that contains a root or prefix, use the dictionary or context to verify your hunch. Sometimes word elements, like

content, communicate only a vague definition, so this extra step may be necessary and helpful to you in your quest to understand a word and a sentence.

In Reading A, "The Pill That Transformed America," you came across several words that contain word elements. You may be familiar with some of these words, such as *anti-contraception.* Even if you have never heard of *anti-contraception,* you can easily get an idea of what the word means. Most students know that the prefix *anti-* means "against" and *contraception* has something to do with preventing pregnancy. From these two pieces of information, you can conclude that *anti-contraception* has something to do with being against devices that prevent pregnancy. You might even go a step further and think about which groups or individuals may be against contraception. Are they against every form of contraception? What is the difference between artificial and natural contraception? Reading A focuses on the development of the birth control pill during the 1950s. Would the groups who were against the pill then be against it now? If you really want to know a word conceptually, these kinds of questions are important to think about.

In the Building Blocks section, we discussed how word parts—prefixes, roots, and suffixes—can help you determine the meanings of words. Like other vocabulary strategies, knowledge of word parts provides a piece of information that leads to a better vocabulary. In the next section, Vocabulary Activities, do the Figuring It Out, Practicing It, and Applying It activities for Reading A.

Vocabulary Activities

 ### Figuring It Out

A.1 DIRECTIONS: Fourteen of the targeted words from "The Pill That Transformed America" contain prefixes or suffixes. On the lines below, write the word first; write its prefix, suffix, or both; then write the meaning of the prefix and/or suffix. You might also want to make vocabulary cards for each of these words.

Word	*Prefix/Suffix/Both*	*Meaning*
1. _____	_____	_____
2. _____	_____	_____

	Word	*Prefix/Suffix/Both*	*Meaning*
3.	_____	_____	_____
4.	_____	_____	_____
5.	_____	_____	_____
6.	_____	_____	_____
7.	_____	_____	_____
8.	_____	_____	_____
9.	_____	_____	_____
10.	_____	_____	_____
11.	_____	_____	_____
12.	_____	_____	_____
13.	_____	_____	_____
14.	_____	_____	_____

A.2 DIRECTIONS: Write the targeted word from Reading A in the blank following the word's definition. Be sure to return to the reading so that you can let the context help you determine the meaning of each word.

1. Which word means "a doctor who specializes in the health care of women"?

_____

2. Which word means "a period of ten years"? _____

3. Which word means "something that can be seen or watched"?

_____

4. Which word describes "someone who is against the use of birth control"?

_____

5. Which word means "legal proceedings"? _____

6. Which word means "someone who studies the science of life and living organisms"? _____

7. Which word means "of or relating to the art of preparing and dispensing drugs"? _____

8. Which word describes "someone who is widely known"? _____

9. Which word means the "intentional prevention of pregnancy with various devices"? _____

10. Which word means "one who gives aid, especially financial aid."

   _____

11. Which word comes from the Latin *pro*, meaning "in favor of," and *gestare*, meaning "to bear"? _____

12. Which word means "a psychological condition characterized by sadness, dejection, and hopelessness"? _____

13. Which word means "the act of discharging eggs from the ovary"?

   _____

14. Which word means "not forcing someone or something inappropriately"?

   _____

15. Which word means "a negative reaction occurring during an illness or as a result of medication"? _____

 ## Practicing It

A.3 DIRECTIONS: Answer the following questions, making sure to provide enough detail to demonstrate your understanding of the boldfaced words. The answers can be found in Reading A, so if you have trouble answering any of the questions, you might want to return to the article.

1. In their search for a *nonintrusive* method of birth control, Sanger and McCormick needed both a *biologist* and a *gynecologist.* Why do you think they needed individuals from both backgrounds?

   _____

   _____

2. What role does the hormone *progesterone* play in preventing *contraception?*

   _____

   _____

3. Why is the pill the most *prominent* form of birth control in spite of all the *complications?*

   _____

   _____

4. How does the pill keep a woman from *ovulating?*

   _____

   _____

5. Why might Massachusetts have been an *anti-contraception* state? Do you think it still is? Why or why not?

   _____

   _____

6. The first oral *contraceptive* trials had *spectacular* results. Why were these results so *spectacular?*

   _____

   _____

7. Give two reasons why you think that it took only a *decade* to get FDA approval for this *pharmaceutical*.

_____

_____

8. Would a *benefactor* of the oral *contraceptive* file *litigation* against its use? Why or why not?

_____

_____

9. Why might a woman stop taking the pill if *depression* was one of the *complications*?

_____

_____

Applying It

A.4 DIRECTIONS: Knowing word parts can help you determine the meaning of unknown words. Each of the words in this exercise is related to one of the targeted words in Reading A but means something different. Use each of these new words in a sentence. Feel free to consult with your classmates or to refer to a dictionary.

1. complicate _____

2. litigator _____

3. intrusive _____

4. conceive _____

5. benefit _____

6. decathlon _____

7. depressed _____

8. pharmacology _____

9. spectacle _____

10. biosphere _____

11. ovum _____

12. gynecology _____

13. prominence _____

14. gestation _____

15. antisocial _____

READING B

Reading B, entitled "Television," focuses on the race to acquire the patent on the invention that we know as television. As you read the article, pay particular attention to the 20 boldfaced words. Some of the targeted words have roots, prefixes, or suffixes, but some do not. See if you can identify those that have roots, prefixes, or suffixes. Before reading the article and completing the Vocabulary Activities, evaluate your present understanding of each of the 20 targeted words. Circle 1, 2, or 3 to indicate how familiar you are with each word (see page 4 for an explanation of the rating system).

	Level of Understanding		
converted	1	2	3
depicted	1	2	3
devised	1	2	3
émigré	1	2	3
harrow	1	2	3
incremental	1	2	3
infrastructure	1	2	3
interactive	1	2	3

litter	1	2	3
mesh	1	2	3
patronage	1	2	3
photosensitive	1	2	3
prodigy	1	2	3
royalties	1	2	3
savvy	1	2	3
scrabbled	1	2	3
sibling	1	2	3
synchronized	1	2	3
tinker	1	2	3
unprecedented	1	2	3

Television

by Adam Rogers

How the tube was born out of a struggle between an Iowa farm boy and a wealthy entrepreneur.

The first commercial television broadcast in America happened exactly where and when it should have—at the 1939 World's Fair in New York. That fair has been called the beginning of the future—it featured freeways, computers, robots and an opening speech by President Franklin D. Roosevelt that was televised to the few hundred television sets in the New York area at the time. A decade later there were 7 million sets in the United States.

But television didn't begin at the World's Fair. It entered the public imagination as early as 1879, when *Punch* cartoonist George du Maurier **depicted** a "telephonoscope" over the mantel of a well-heeled couple. The idea was an easy extension of the two hip **interactive** media of the day—the telephone and the telegraph. If it worked for sound, why not pictures? In the end, though, the invention of television came down to a race, and a contest of wills, between two men: Philo Farnsworth, a self-taught electrical engineer from an Iowa farm, and David Sarnoff, the tech-**savvy** marketer who started NBC.

Perhaps they should share a bit of the credit with a third man, the creator of one of those brilliant false starts that *litter* the history of invention. In 1883 a German engineer named Paul Nipkow *devised* what he called the Nipkow disk. The disk was pierced with small holes arranged on a spiral, and had a light source positioned behind it. When the disk was spun, light shining through the holes would streak across a picture, one light per hole. Those lines could be *converted* into electrical signals and transmitted to another Nipkow disk, which could in turn reconstruct the original picture on a *photosensitive* surface. At first, the system looked good for sending copies of documents—an early fax machine. But it seemed it would work for moving pictures as well.

The problem was that the disks had to be precisely *synchronized* and spin very fast—the system tended to become unstable. So as far back as 1908, engineers were trying to figure out an all-electronic system that would scan images with "cathode rays," streams of electrons in a vacuum tube. But how to direct the beam onto the thing you're trying to take a picture of, or onto the photosensitive screen for display?

That's where Farnsworth came in. A farm boy who didn't see electricity until he was 12 years old, he proved to be something of a *prodigy* after discovering a stack of old technical magazines and a Delco farm generator to *tinker* with. In the summer of 1921, when Farnsworth was 14, he turned a horse-drawn *harrow* around at the edge of a hayfield he'd just mowed and looked at the neat lines crossing the cut grass. Farnsworth realized that magnetic fields could direct a beam of electrons across an image, one line at a time, and that the resulting signals, fired at an electron-sensitive screen, would *mesh* so fast that the human eye would perceive a continuous picture. Over the next 20 years, Farnsworth *scrabbled* for funding and lab space while he made *incremental* improvements in his device. His wife worked with him; his brother-in-law became an expert glass blower to make the vacuum tubes they needed. They had a working model by 1928.

While Farnsworth and his family were tinkering in a tiny room in San Francisco, Vladimir Zworykin, a Russian *émigré,* was working on cathode-ray tubes in a well-funded, well-staffed lab in New York. Zworykin, too, was able to come up with a working electronic television, and he had the advantage of the *patronage* of his employer, David Sarnoff of RCA. Sarnoff was a genius when it came to seeing the potential in a technology; he was the first to suggest radios for home use and a network of stations to broadcast to them. And he knew this television thing was going places.

Zworykin's work was arguably behind Farnsworth's, but that didn't suit Sarnoff. His motto was "RCA doesn't pay *royalties.* It collects them." By the 1930s, Sarnoff—through Zworykin—and Farnsworth were fighting it out in the patent courts. Farnsworth ended up with six basic television patents, but Sarnoff had an ace: The National Broadcasting Co., or NBC, a radio network that could offer the *infrastructure* for a *sibling* television network.

By 1951 color televisions went on sale. Broadcasters like Dave Garroway and Ernie Kovacs were beginning to define the content of television as we know it today. And the invention clearly isn't finished. Digital television will—we're told—offer pictures of **unprecedented** clarity and allow a seamless connection with a newer mass medium, the Internet. Maybe the technology will be ready in time for the next world's fair. ■

Comprehension Quick-Check

After reading "Television," ask your instructor for a copy of the Comprehension Quick-Check Quiz.

Vocabulary Activities

 Figuring It Out

B.1 DIRECTIONS: Using your dictionary to help you out if necessary, circle the correct definition of each boldfaced word. Before you make your selection, be sure to return to Reading B and see how the word is used in context. To help you learn the words, you may want to make vocabulary cards, as described in Chapter 2.

1. ". . . lines could be **converted** into electrical signals . . ."
   a. sent
   b. dispatched
   c. transmitted
   d. changed

2. ". . . George du Maurier **depicted** a 'telephonoscope' . . ."
   a. decided on
   b. represented
   c. drew
   d. suggested

3. ". . . Paul Nipkow **devised** what he called the Nipkow disk."
   a. developed
   b. supported
   c. induced
   d. predicted

4. "...Vladimir Zworykin, a Russian *émigré*..."
   a. worker
   b. stowaway
   c. criminal
   d. emigrant

5. "...he turned a horse-drawn *harrow* around at the edge of a hayfield..."
   a. hand cart
   b. wheel barrow
   c. plow
   d. carriage

6. "...while he made *incremental* improvements..."
   a. steady
   b. unnoticed
   c. suggested
   d. odd

7. "...offer the *infrastructure* for a sibling television network."
   a. advertising
   b. funding
   c. foundation
   d. personnel

8. "...the two hip *interactive* media of the day..."
   a. offering two-way communication
   b. digital
   c. most popular
   d. dramatic

9. "...false starts that *litter* the history of invention."
   a. undermine
   b. clarify
   c. are scattered throughout
   d. clog

10. "...would *mesh* so fast that the human eye would perceive..."
    a. break apart
    b. stabilize
    c. fit together
    d. trick

11. "... the advantage of the ***patronage*** of his employer ..."
    a. customers
    b. encouragement
    c. opinion
    d. suggestions

12. "... construct the original picture on a ***photosensitive*** surface."
    a. sensitive to light
    b. sensitive to heat
    c. sensitive to motion
    d. sensitive to sound

13. "... he proved to be something of a ***prodigy*** ..."
    a. a person who knows a lot about electronics
    b. a person who reads a lot
    c. a person who has exceptional talents
    d. a person who has saved a considerable amount of money

14. "... 'RCA doesn't pay ***royalties.***'"
    a. salaries to high-ranking executives
    b. payments for the right to use a product
    c. agreed-upon amounts of money paid for a service provided
    d. biweekly salaries

15. "... the tech-***savvy*** marketer ..."
    a. stupid
    b. book smart
    c. well informed
    d. uneducated

16. "... Farnsworth ***scrabbled*** for funding ..."
    a. doing something in a quick, disorderly way
    b. made an informed decision
    c. struggled to find an answer to a problem
    d. asked family and friends to provide financial support

17. "... offer the infrastructure for a ***sibling*** television network."
    a. new-found
    b. existing
    c. competitive
    d. related

18. "... disks had to be precisely *synchronized* and spin very fast ..."
    a. parallel to one another
    b. operating in unison
    c. moving at the same speed
    d. giving the identical message

19. "... a Delco farm generator to *tinker* with."
    a. unskillfully work on something
    b. destroy accidentally
    c. repair a broken machine
    d. throw away something that is no longer useful

20. "... offer pictures of *unprecedented* clarity ..."
    a. rarely occurring
    b. accidental
    c. occurring naturally
    d. never before occurring

Practicing It

B.2 DIRECTIONS: Read each sentence carefully. Circle *Y* if the answer to the question is yes. Circle *N* if the answer to the question is no. Then briefly explain your answer, making sure to provide enough detail to demonstrate your understanding of the boldfaced words.

Y   N   1. Would a *savvy* student wait until the night before an exam to begin studying?

_____

Y   N   2. If you and your friends *synchronized* your watches, would your watches *depict* exactly the same time?

_____

Y   N   3. If you received *royalties* in *unprecedented* amounts, would you consider sharing them with your *siblings*?

_____

Y   N   **4.** Do motion control devices demonstrate *photosensitivity*?

_____

Y   N   **5.** Would an *émigré* who is a *prodigy* stand a good chance of being successful in the United States?

_____

Y   N   **6.** Would *meshing* two or more data sets be all but impossible on the computers being made today?

_____

Y   N   **7.** Would a restaurant that has to *scrabble* for *patronage* be open very long?

_____

B . 3   D I R E C T I O N S : Complete each of the following sentences with one of the targeted words from Reading B.

8. A city should repair its _____ before everything starts to fall apart.

9. _____ video games can be good learning devices for even very small children.

10. One of the basic operations in mathematics is knowing how to _____ fractions into decimals and decimals into fractions.

11. Like print material such as magazines and newspapers, the Internet is _____(ed) with advertisements that try to persuade you to buy a new product or try a new service.

12. If you make _____ deposits to a good investment fund, by the time you retire, you should be able to have a high quality of living standard.

13. Farmers use a _____ to break up and level the ground before planting their crops.

14. My grandmother used to say, "Don't _____ with success!" What she meant was, "Don't mess things up when they are going well!"

15. The person who _____ the first computer, which was very large in size and limited in capabilities, would probably be amazed at how small computers are today and how fast they operate.

Applying It

B.4 DIRECTIONS: Complete each of the following analogies with one of the targeted words from Reading B. Be sure to think about the relationship between the completed word pair before you fill in the missing word.

1. *depict* : show :: _____ : invent

2. CD player : audio equipment :: _____ : farm machinery

3. brilliant : _____ :: sister : *sibling*

4. *converted* : garage :: _____ : message

5. spend : _____ :: *tinker* : car

6. restaurant : _____ :: school : students

B.5 DIRECTIONS: Circle the item that is *not* an example of the bold-faced word.

7. *Infrastructure*: highways, bridges, department stores, sewer systems

8. Things that can be *synchronized*: swimmers, watches, class periods, messages

9. *Savvy* people: smart shoppers, cheaters, consistent savers, planners

10. *Interactive* things: video games, telephones, the Internet, radios

11. Things that you can *mesh*: pens, files, ideas, paragraphs

12. Things that are *incremental*: pay raises, savings accounts, weight gain, weather changes

13. Reasons why you might have to *scrabble* for money: you are rich; payday is a week away; you are trying to open your own business; you want to buy your first home

14. Things an *émigré* from Asia might have to do: learn a new language, leave family members behind, change religion, adapt to a different culture

READING C

Reading C, entitled "The Anatomy of Stress," focuses on the damage that everyday stress, accumulated over many years, can do to the human body. Think about times when you felt stressed. How did your body feel? How do you know when you are stressed? What types of events cause you to feel stressed? As you read the article, pay particular attention to the 25 targeted words. Some of them have roots, prefixes, or suffixes, but some do not. Also, four of these words that have to do specifically with medicine and science have been isolated for you. These words have roots. Before reading the article and completing the Vocabulary Activities, evaluate your present understanding of each of the 25 targeted words. Circle 1, 2, or 3 to indicate how familiar you are with each word (see page 4 for an explanation of the rating system).

	Level of Understanding		
acute	1	2	3
buffering	1	2	3
chaotic	1	2	3
cohesive	1	2	3
commensurately	1	2	3
elevated	1	2	3
empirical	1	2	3

harboring	1	2	3
holistic	1	2	3
impinge	1	2	3
mantra	1	2	3
metabolized	1	2	3
mobilizing	1	2	3
modulate	1	2	3
obesity	1	2	3
orthodox	1	2	3
plaques	1	2	3
predator	1	2	3
quantifiable	1	2	3
spawned	1	2	3
wreaks	1	2	3

Words from Science

adrenaline	1	2	3
endocrinologist	1	2	3
epidemiology	1	2	3
psychoneuroimmunology	1	2	3

The Anatomy of Stress   by Jerry Adler

Stress isn't just a catchall complaint; it's being linked to heart disease, immune deficiency and memory loss. We're learning that men and women process stress differently and that childhood stress can lead to adult health problems. The worst part is, we inflict it on ourselves.

Some people make a virtue of stress, under the **mantra** "that which does not kill me makes me stronger." But science shows this to be a lie. A whole new body of research shows the damage stress **wreaks** on the body: not just heart disease and ulcers, but loss of memory, diminished immune function and even a particular type of **obesity.** That which doesn't kill you, it turns out, really does kill you in the end, but first it makes you fat.

Zen masters, of course, have known this for a long time, and techniques such as yoga are still useful prescriptions for stress. But **orthodox** Western medicine long resisted the notion that a purely mental condition could have measurable effects in the **empirical** realm of arteries and organs. It was only in the past few years that researchers came up with a **quantifiable** measure of stress, based on the concentration of certain hormones in saliva, and began tracing the complex neurological and chemical events that lead from a traffic jam on the Santa Monica Freeway to cardiac intensive care at Cedars-Sinai. Research has revealed that men's and women's bodies process stress differently, and provided disturbing evidence about how stress affects child development from the earliest weeks of life. And it has **spawned** a whole new discipline, **psychoneuroimmunology**—which, according to Bruce Rabin of the University of Pittsburgh, has reached the point where research on smoking and cancer was back in the 1960s. "You knew there was a link because of the **epidemiology,** but you didn't know the mechanism. Now there's enough epidemiology to establish the association [between stress and illness]. We're still working out the mechanisms."

The very concept of stress was formulated only in the 1930s, by the pioneering **endocrinologist** Hans Selye. It was Selye's insight that organisms show a common biological response to a wide range of unpleasant sensory or psychological experiences. These are called "stressors." Stressors are, in shorthand, whatever you're trying to avoid: an electric shock, if you're a lab rat; the sight of a **predator,** if you're a prey animal; a 500-point drop in the Dow, if you're a Yuppie. Those are **acute** stress events; everyone recognizes the **adrenaline** rush (pounding heart, dry mouth, butterflies in the stomach) that marks their onset. Human beings are equipped to deal with it, if it doesn't happen too often. But when it happens again and again, the effects multiply and cascade, invisibly, compounding over a lifetime.

Yet the stress reaction obviously serves an evolutionary purpose. It is, essentially, a response to danger, in two distinct phases. The first of these, involving the "sympathetic-adreno-medullary axis" (SAM), is the familiar flight-or-fight response. Your brain perceives a threat—a lion crouched in the brush is the classic illustration—and sends a message down the spinal cord to the medulla, or core, of the adrenal glands, signaling it to pump out adrenaline. In a matter of seconds, the body is transformed. To prepare for exertion, blood pressure and heart rate skyrocket; the liver pours out glucose and calls up fat reserves to be processed into triglycerides for energy; the circulatory system diverts blood from nonessential functions, such as digestion, to the brain and muscles. This is precisely what you need if your goal is to survive the next 10 minutes.

Civilization, by contrast, gives you the opportunity to experience an adrenaline rush at every traffic light. And—since all you're doing is sitting in your car—the elaborate preparations your body makes are wasted. Worse than wasted: every heartbeat at **elevated** blood pressure takes its toll on the arteries. The excess fats and glucose don't get **metabolized** right away, so they stay in the bloodstream. The fats contribute to the **plaques** that form inside blood vessels, which can lead to heart disease or strokes; high levels of glucose are a step in the direction of diabetes.

And amazingly enough, stress can even change the shape of your body. Since the stress reaction involves **mobilizing** the body's fat reserves for energy, Peeke says, it makes sense to store that fat near the liver, which processes it so it can be metabolized in the muscles. Sure enough, fat cells in the abdomen appear to be especially sensitive to glucocorticoids, and people with a high concentration of those hormones tend to accumulate fat around their middles—a potbelly—even if the rest of their bodies are thin. Researchers think that waist–hip ratio, the relative circumference of those two body parts, could be a useful way to identify people at risk for stress-related disease.

Catherine Stoney of Ohio State has also found significant differences between men and women. Women's blood pressure goes up less than men's in reaction to stress (although their response increases noticeably after menopause or hysterectomy, suggesting a **buffering** effect from estrogen). But women tend to react to a wider range of outside stressors than men, according to Ronald Kessler of Harvard, who asked 166 married couples to keep a daily stress diary for six weeks. Women feel stress more often, says Kessler, because they take a **holistic** view of everyday life. A man may worry if someone in his immediate family is sick; his wife takes on the burdens of the whole neighborhood. "Men take care of one thing [at a time]," he says. "Women put the pieces together again."

Apart from gender, early childhood experiences seem to have a powerful influence on how people deal with stress. Children raised in orphanages or in neglectful homes may have elevated levels of glucocorticoids and "hot" responses to stress later in life. "We're finding," says Frank Treiber of the Medical College of Georgia, "that if you come from a family that's somewhat **chaotic,** unstable, not **cohesive, harboring** grudges, very early on, it's associated later with greater blood-pressure reactivity to various types of stress." The brains of children up to around the age of 8 are still developing in response to the environment; cells literally live or die as experiences **impinge** on it. "The early brain can become hard-wired to deal with high fear states," says Dr. Jay Giedd of the National Institutes of Health. "Its normal state will be to have a lot of adrenaline flowing. When these children become adults they'll feel empty or bored if they're not on edge." Contrariwise, children raised in secure, loving homes learn to **modulate** the stress reaction, according to Megan Gunnar of the University of Minnesota. As early as three months, well-cared-for babies can suffer discomfort without evoking a stress response; they'll cry when they get a physical exam, but their stress hormones don't go up ***commensurately.*** "Children who are in secure, emotionally support-ive relationships are buffered to everyday stressors," she says. ■

Comprehension Quick-Check

After reading "The Anatomy of Stress," ask your instructor for a copy of the Com-prehension Quick-Check Quiz.

Vocabulary Activities

 ## Figuring It Out

C.1 DIRECTIONS: Match a word from the list of targeted words in "Anatomy of Stress" with each definition. To help learn the words more easily, you may wish to make vocabulary cards so that you can include all the important infor-mation about each word.

Targeted Word	*Definition*
1. _____	sticking with beliefs that are commonly accepted, customary, or traditional
2. _____	increased in amount
3. _____	to adjust or adapt, to regulate
4. _____	severe, intense
5. _____	emphasizing the importance of the whole and the relationship among its parts
6. _____	brings about or causes damage
7. _____	characterized by great disorder or confusion
8. _____	to advance beyond acceptable limits

	Targeted Word	*Definition*

9. _____ fatty materials lining an artery

10. _____ protecting by absorbing or moderating negative influences

11. _____ the condition of being extremely fat

12. _____ gave rise to, started, promoted

13. _____ something that lives by attacking other organisms

14. _____ corresponding in proportion or degree

15. _____ information that relies on or is proven from observation or experimentation

16. _____ expressible as a measurable amount or quantity

17. _____ subjected to the chemical processes that enable a cell and an organism to live

18. _____ having or entertaining a thought or feeling

19. _____ preparing for, readying

20. _____ having parts that stick together

21. _____ a verbal statement that is repeated in meditation or prayer

C.2 **DIRECTIONS:** Using what you learned about word parts in the last chapter and what you learned about context clues, write a definition of each of the words from science.

22. epidemiology _____

23. adrenaline _____

24. endocrinologist _____

25. psychoneuroimmunology _____

Practicing It

C.3 DIRECTIONS: Answer each question by circling all of the choices that apply to the boldfaced word. For some questions, all of the choices may be correct. For others, there may be only one correct response.

1. Which of the following might suffer from *obesity*?
   a. a dog who will eat anything she can sink her teeth into
   b. a child who eats lots of candy and other sweets
   c. a newborn kitten whose mother was killed by a car
   d. a teenager who eats a well-balanced diet

2. Which of the following could be *cohesive*?
   a. a family
   b. several good friends
   c. predators
   d. a letter to an employer about a job opportunity

3. Which of the following would cause *acute* pain?
   a. the prick of a very sharp needle
   b. a small splinter
   c. elevated feet
   d. childbirth

4. Which of the following would be considered an *empirical* study with *quantifiable* results?
   a. A researcher examines the relationship between weight and the occurrence of heart attacks.
   b. A researcher takes notes about the habits of gorillas and keeps a journal describing these habits.
   c. A researcher has two groups of students use different study techniques and then compares their test performance.
   d. A historian writes a new book about what happened during the Vietnam War.

5. Which of the following may be blocked by *plaque*, as defined in this article?
   a. teeth
   b. trophy cases
   c. veins
   d. arteries

6. Which of the following might *spawn chaos*?
   a. the stock market losing half of its value in one day
   b. the overthrow of a government
   c. everyone at a company getting an exceptionally large raise in pay
   d. every student in a course receiving a D or an F on an important exam

7. Which of the following could you *harbor*?
   a. the police
   b. a criminal
   c. a hostage
   d. a grudge

C.4 DIRECTIONS: Read each sentence carefully. If the boldfaced word is used correctly, circle *C* and go on to the next item. If the boldfaced word is used incorrectly, circle *I* and then make the sentence correct.

C I **8.** Because her body couldn't *metabolize* dairy products, every time Caroline drank milk it *wreaked* havoc on her stomach and intestinal tract.

C I **9.** When a job advertisement reads "Salary *commensurate* with experience," the company expects that all applicants will have little experience and will work for low wages.

C I **10.** Today, we consider the use of leeches to heal a wound to be *orthodox* medical care.

C I **11.** You can be fairly certain that a new law that is seen as *impinging* on the rights of a certain group of people will be challenged in court.

C I **12.** When Calvin decided to approach the problem from a *holistic* perspective, he divided the problem into small parts and examined each part separately.

C I **13.** A *buffer* zone is often used outside an abortion clinic to *modulate* the tension between the clinic and protesters.

C I **14.** If you are attacked by a *predator*, your body tends to *mobilize* its defenses by giving you power or energy you wouldn't normally have.

Applying It

C.5 DIRECTIONS: Select from the list of targeted words for Reading C a word that is the *antonym*, or opposite, of the word listed below.

	Targeted Word	*Antonym*
1.	_____	thinness
2.	_____	divided, in separate parts
3.	_____	finished, brought to an end
4.	_____	not intense, mild
5.	_____	backing down, disbanding
6.	_____	turning loose
7.	_____	nontraditional

C.6 DIRECTIONS: For each of the following items, give an example that demonstrates your understanding of the boldfaced word.

8. A mouse's *predator*

_____

9. Behavior that *impinges* on the rights of others

_____

10. An individual who might have an *elevated* cholesterol level

_____

11. Something that is both *quantifiable* and *empirical*

_____

12. Two jobs for which you might be paid *commensurately* with your experience

_____

13. Why you might need an *endocrinologist*

_____

14. A building or some other place that might have a *buffer* zone

_____

15. A *mantra* for someone who is *obese* and is sincere about losing weight

_____

16. Something that *wreaks* havoc on people who are constantly under stress

_____

17. Something you might do to *modulate* the amount of *plaque* in the arteries in your heart

_____

18. Something that would cause your body to release *adrenaline*

_____

19. A situation in which it might be important to examine someone's medical problems from a *holistic* viewpoint

_____

20. Something that might happen to your health if your job is constantly *chaotic.*

_____

21. Something you couldn't eat if your body failed to *metabolize* protein

_____

22. Something you would study if you were an *epidemiologist*

_____

▶ Extending

DIRECTIONS: Using the lists of prefixes, suffixes, and roots that are provided in Chapter 4, figure out the meaning of each of the targeted words below, and write a meaningful definition in each blank. If you are unsure of the word's meaning, consult your dictionary to help you. Remember, it's important to use as many sources as it takes so that you can have a clear meaning of these words.

1. matriarchy _____

2. sonorous _____

3. pseudonym _____

4. transatlantic _____

5. compliant _____

6. radiology _____

7. carnivore _____

8. biodegradable _____

9. cognition _____

10. vocation _____

11. neurologist _____

12. contraband _____

13. counterproductive _____

14. incredible _____

15. podiatrist _____

Evaluating

Review and test yourself on the 60 targeted words in this chapter. Then ask your instructor for the comprehensive exam on these words.

Summary

In this chapter we present the advantages of using word elements as you learn vocabulary generatively. Prefixes, suffixes, and roots can be quite beneficial in adding to the information you need to know. Knowledge of word elements can also be useful as you search for words in your dictionaries. We recommend that your understanding of word elements be supported by the dictionary and by the context provided by the writer/author of what you are reading. When these three pieces of the puzzle are placed together, you will be well on your way to broadening and improving your conceptual vocabulary knowledge.

PART II

Additional Readings and Practice Activities

In Part I we presented numerous strategies that can help you learn words in a generative way. By *generative* we mean that you now have the necessary tools to figure out and learn the meanings of new words on your own. No longer will you skip or read over words that you don't know or words for which you have only a vague meaning. Because you know what it means to learn a word conceptually and the generative strategies to accomplish this task, your ability to comprehend and grasp meaning should also improve.

Part II is designed to give you additional practice in honing your vocabulary skills and to introduce you to more words that may be unfamiliar to you. Each of the three chapters in Part II contains three selections on which you can practice. As a general rule, the first reading in each chapter is shorter than the other two and has fewer words for you to learn. Each reading is formatted in the following way:

Self-Evaluation—As in Part I, you evaluate your current level of understanding of each targeted word by circling 1, 2, or 3 before reading the article.

Reading (A, B, or C)—Each chapter contains three selections. It is important to read each one so that you can see how the targeted (bold-faced) words are used in context.

Comprehension Quick-Check—After you read each selection, you will need to see your instructor for a copy of the Comprehension Quick-Check Quiz. This step is important so that you can be sure you understood what you read.

Building Blocks Revisited—The Building Blocks feature has been carried over into Part II. As in Part I, in this section we offer ideas and strategies to help you learn the targeted words.

Figuring It Out—As in Part I, these activities help you learn the Stage 1 aspect of the targeted word.

Practicing It—As in Part I, these activities help you learn the Stage 2 aspect of the targeted word.

Applying It—As in Part I, these activities help you learn the Stage 3 aspect, or the conceptual level, of the targeted word. Your goal is to learn each word at this level.

Extending (only with Reading C)—These activities help you stretch your vocabulary knowledge. The words in the Extending activities are drawn from any of the three readings in the chapter.

Evaluating—See your instructor for the final evaluation for the words in all three readings. These evaluation activities have a variety of formats.

We believe that if you practice your new-found skills in the last three chapters of this book, you will be ready to meet the challenges of learning and using new words in your daily life. Keep in mind that when you learn words conceptually, you can correctly use them in your conversations and in your writing, and you will have a clear understanding of what they mean when you come across them in your reading.

5 Practice 1

DID YOU KNOW?

The word *chauvinism* originated from Nicolas Chauvin, a Frenchman, who was an extreme believer in Napoleon and his causes. Today the word applies to anyone who is unreasonably prejudiced about a cause.

READING A

Perhaps you saw the movie *When Harry Met Sally*, starring Meg Ryan and Tom Hanks. Reading A, which deals with the difficulties that males and females have in relating to each other, plays upon the title of that movie. The author suggests that men and women experience difficulties because they do not communicate in the same manner. Before reading the article and completing the Vocabulary Activities, evaluate your present understanding of each of the 13 targeted words. Circle 1, 2, or 3 to indicate how familiar you are with each word (see page 4 for an explanation of the rating system).

Level of Understanding

averted	1	2	3
condescension	1	2	3
consolation	1	2	3
decipher	1	2	3
disparate	1	2	3
distinctions	1	2	3
dominance	1	2	3
endowed	1	2	3

enhance	1	2	3
inclined	1	2	3
inferiority	1	2	3
instinctively	1	2	3
phenomenon	1	2	3

When Harry Called Sally . . .
Why Men and Women Can't Communicate   *by Jerry Adler*

When Sylvia found out she was pregnant, she couldn't wait to call her mother and spend hours on the phone planning for the new baby. Her husband, Marvin, on the other hand, put off calling his own parents until the weekend, when it was cheaper, and then spent 25 minutes talking to his father about a problem he was having with his gun. Finally his father asked what else was new.

"Nothing much with me," he replied, "but Sylvia's pregnant."

Men! Or, to put it another way, women! The only two creatures on God's good earth **endowed** with the miracle of speech—by what mishap of evolution did they end up putting it to such **disparate,** indeed, conflicting, uses? This is a question for "sociolinguists," whatever they are, and Deborah Tannen, who is one, explores it in her bestseller, *You Just Don't Understand: Women and Men in Conversation.* . . . Sylvia was using language to **enhance** *intimacy,* by sharing her feelings about pregnancy with her mother. Marvin, on the other hand, was defending his *independence* by distancing himself from the pregnancy, avoiding any discussion of his feelings. If only Sylvia and Marvin had understood these universal **distinctions.** Sylvia might never have moved back to her parents' house and Marvin's subsequent alcohol and legal problems might well have been **averted.***

Alberta and Murray are driving from Teaneck, N.J., to her cousin's wedding in Connecticut. They have been lost in the Bronx for half an hour, and Murray has just turned onto the Cross Bronx Expressway.

Alberta: I think we're headed back to New Jersey.

Murray: No, this is right.

Alberta: We seem to be going west.

Murray: Don't be ridiculous. What makes you think we're going west?

*The anecdotes in this article are not drawn from Tannen's book.

Alberta: Well, the sun is going down in front of us.

Murray (slams on the brakes): Well, if you don't care for the way I'm driving, you can try walking to your fat cousin's stupid wedding!

Who is right in this situation?

Alberta, focused on the goal of getting to the wedding, failed to consider that Murray would take her remark about the sun as a criticism of his ability to find the Merritt Parkway. The problem, in Tannen's theory, is that men and women use language differently. Women take the attitude that the purpose of a conversation is to explore cooperative solutions to common problems, while men regard speech as an extension of fighting by other means. So strong is the urge to **dominance** in American men that they will drive right past a policeman rather than stop and ask for directions, because to ask for help is to put oneself in a position of **inferiority.** By contrast, according to Tannen, American women are so accustomed to asking for help that they have been known to ask strangers for directions *even when they know perfectly well where they are going.*

All over America, couples are waking up to insights such as these. American marriages may never be the same, once spouses learn to **decipher** the "metamessages" men and women send to one another. Tannen's research has led her to the discovery that men hate to be told to do anything. She uses this principle to explain the **phenomenon** known to sociolinguists as *nagging.* "A woman," she writes, "will be **inclined** to repeat a request that doesn't get a response because she is convinced that her husband would do what she asks if he only understood that she really wants him to do it. But a man who wants to avoid feeling that he is following orders may **instinctively** wait before doing what she asked, in order to imagine that he is doing it of his own free will. Nagging is the result, because each time she repeats the request, he again puts off fulfilling it."

Edna: What's bothering you, honey?

George: Nothin'.

Edna: Something's bothering you, I can tell.

George: Nothin's bothering me.

Edna: Yes, it is.

George: Why do you think something's bothering me?

Edna: Well, for one thing, you're bleeding all over your shirt.

George: It doesn't bother me.

Edna: WELL, IT BOTHERS THE HELL OUT OF ME!

George: I'll go change my shirt.

In this case, Edna's effort to get her husband to talk about his bleeding was interpreted by him as a kind of **condescension,** implying that he is incapable of dealing with the situation himself. For the same reason that they refuse to ask for directions, men resist the intimacy of discussing their feelings, because it implies a need for help, advice, or **consolation.** By offering to change his shirt, George could present himself as meeting his wife's literal demand ("get that bloody thing out of my sight") without responding to her deeper need for a discussion of why he was bleeding in the first place, and how he felt about it.

Men! Or, to look at it from the opposite point of view, women! Whatever gave them the idea of living together? ■

Comprehension Quick-Check

After reading "When Harry Called Sally . . . ," ask your instructor for a copy of the Comprehension Quick-Check Quiz.

Building Blocks Revisited

We recommend that you make a vocabulary card for each of the 13 targeted words. Because some of them are particularly challenging, you may wish to use additional vocabulary strategies. For example, your understanding of the word *disparate* is probably at Stage 1 or Stage 2. As mentioned in Chapter 2, one way to learn the meanings of words that are difficult and unknown to you is to use the keyword strategy. With the word *disparate,* you might try this:

> In the word *disparate* you can see the small word *par,* a word familiar to a golfer. Imagine that you are a golfer and you never can achieve *par* on any hole. You would obviously become *discouraged.* The letters *dis-* begin the word *disparate.* So you can imagine a golfer who never receives a *par* who becomes *discouraged* because his game is so distinct and dissimilar from the games of his friends who score lower and better. The meaning of *disparate* is distinct and dissimilar.

Try developing a keyword strategy for any of the other targeted words that you are having difficulty in learning. For example, the word *phenomenon* may be initially troublesome. What smaller words do you see in this word that could create a story similar to the golfing story?

Put your keyword strategies on the front of your vocabulary cards.

Some of the other words use important word elements. As mentioned in Chapter 4, word elements can often help you determine the meaning of a word. In addition, word elements can help you remember the definition. As you look up these words in the dictionary, pay particular attention to their roots or suffixes: ***averted, dominance, inclined,*** and ***inferiority.*** In addition, make sure you notice that the word ***inclined*** is a multiple-meaning word. You will need to select the dictionary definition of ***inclined*** that fits the context of the article. Once you have created vocabulary cards and used any other appropriate strategies, complete the three Vocabulary Activities.

Vocabulary Activities

 ## Figuring It Out

A.1 DIRECTIONS: Fill in each blank with the appropriate targeted word from Reading A.

Targeted Word	*Definition*
1. _____	prevented, avoided
2. _____	to increase
3. _____	differences
4. _____	an occurrence that you can sense
5. _____	the condition of being lower in quality or value
6. _____	comfort
7. _____	having a tendency or preference
8. _____	equipped or supplied with
9. _____	not similar
10. _____	to read or interpret
11. _____	naturally without thinking
12. _____	needless, insulting superior behavior
13. _____	the condition of being in control

Practicing It

A.2 DIRECTIONS: Read each sentence carefully. If the boldfaced word is used correctly, circle *C* and go on to the next item. If the boldfaced word is used incorrectly, circle *I* and then make the sentence correct.

C I 1. The eager student tried to *enhance* his worldly knowledge by reading the *New York Times* and several magazines on a weekly basis.

C I 2. The elderly woman *averted* financial disaster when she invested her life savings with the con artist.

C I 3. The large male gorilla had gained *dominance* over the female and younger male gorillas who inhabited the forest with him.

C I 4. The dropout who had not learned how to read quickly *deciphered* the letter from his lawyer.

C I 5. The proud and hardworking couple welcomed the *condescension* of their wealthy landlord, who had inherited his fortune from his grandfather.

C I 6. The husband and wife were so *disparate*; he liked to spend his spare time reading while she sought out parties and crowds of people for socializing.

C I 7. Her feelings of *inferiority* caused her to feel comfortable seeking out new friends and unfamiliar situations.

C I 8. The English professor praised the student on his term paper because he had overlooked the *distinction* between paraphrasing and copying someone's ideas as if they were his own.

C I 9. The *consolation* offered by the minister helped the young woman who had lost her husband in the war.

C I 10. The experienced schoolteacher was *inclined* to be stricter with his rules at the beginning of the school year.

C I 11. The young baseball player was *endowed* with good eye–hand coordination and excellent speed.

C I 12. When the school year began, all the American students in Beginning Russian knew how to speak and write the language *instinctively*.

C I 13. Some companies, such as Nike, have benefited from the *phenomenon* of marking clothes, hats, and shoes with labels or specific color designs.

Applying It

A.3 DIRECTIONS: Answer the following statements, making sure to provide enough detail to demonstrate your understanding of the boldfaced words.

1. Would it be easy to *decipher* a letter written by a two-year-old? Why or why not? _____

   _____

2. Is it easy to like a person who consistently acts in a *condescending* manner? Why or why not? _____

   _____

3. What abilities or skills does a professional baseball player need to be *endowed* with? _____

   _____

4. Describe how someone who suffers from feelings of *inferiority* would act at a social occasion such as a party. _____

   _____

5. Describe how young adults might *enhance* their opportunities to obtain secure, well-paying jobs. _____

   _____

6. Describe how a wise college student might *avert* academic failure or probation. _____

   _____

7. Give an example of an individual who might offer *consolation* to a homeless family. _____

   _____

8. Would the usual clothing worn by a lawyer be *disparate* from the clothing of a heavy metal rock star? Why or why not? _____

_____

9. Is yawning an *instinctive* behavior? Why or why not? _____

_____

10. Describe one *distinction* between football and hockey. _____

_____

11. Would a professor wish to maintain *dominance* in the classroom? Why or why not? _____

_____

12. Would someone *inclined* toward physical activities such as jogging and biking choose to take the elevator or walk the stairs? Why? _____

_____

13. Give an example of a recent medical, scientific, or technological *phenomenon* that has improved your quality of life. _____

_____

READING B

Have you formed an opinion about capital punishment? Whatever your opinion might be, read Reading B carefully because it explains a new test that is releasing many individuals from prison and from the death sentence. Before reading the article and completing the Vocabulary Activities, evaluate your present understanding of each of the 17 targeted words. Circle 1, 2, or 3 to indicate how familiar you are with each word (see page 4 for an explanation of the rating system).

Level of Understanding

bogus	1	2	3
coerced	1	2	3
epilogue	1	2	3
exoneration, exonerated	1	2	3
frantically	1	2	3
inept	1	2	3
lethal	1	2	3
litany	1	2	3
litigation	1	2	3
moratorium	1	2	3
muffle	1	2	3
ratified	1	2	3
shambles (noun)	1	2	3
squandered	1	2	3
status quo	1	2	3
statutory	1	2	3
stay	1	2	3

When Justice Lets Us Down

*by Jim Dwyer, Peter Neufeld,
and Barry Scheck*

It's happening more and more: a convicted criminal, heading for execution, is sprung by DNA tests. And if the innocent are in jail, the guilty are still out there.

Newsweek, February 14, 2000.

The warden was seated at the head of a long table when Ron Williamson was led into the office and told to sit down. Once, Williamson had been a professional baseball player, the hero jock who married the beauty queen in his small Oklahoma town. Now, on an August morning in 1994, at 41, the athlete had passed directly from his prime to a state beyond age. His hair had gone stringy and white; his face had shrunk to a skeletal mask wrapped in pasty, toneless skin.

The warden said he had a duty to carry out, and he read from a piece of paper: You have been sentenced to die by *lethal* injection, and such sentence will be carried out at 12:30 A.M., the 24th of September, 1994. The prison had received no stay of execution, the warden said, so Williamson would be brought to the holding area next to the death chamber until the 24th.

He was led back to a cell, screaming from that moment on, night and day, even after they moved him into another unit with double doors to *muffle* the noise. On Sept. 17, Williamson was shifted into the special cell for prisoners with less than a week to live. By then, the screaming had torn his throat to ribbons, but everyone knew his raspy, desperate *litany:* "I did not rape or kill Debra Sue Carter! I am an innocent man!" In Norman, Okla., a public defender named Janet Chesley *frantically* scrambled a team to move the case into federal court, assembling a mass of papers and fresh arguments. With just five days to go, they won a *stay.*

One year later, U.S. district court Judge Frank Seay would rule that Williamson's trial had been a constitutional *shambles.* His conviction and death sentence—*ratified* by every state court in Oklahoma—had been plagued by unreliable informants, prosecutorial misconduct, an *inept* defense lawyer, *bogus* scientific evidence and a witness who himself was a likely suspect, the federal judge said. He vacated the conviction.

Last April, before Williamson could be tried again, DNA tests arranged by the Innocence Project at the Benjamin N. Cardozo Law School in New York proved that he was actually innocent. Across the country, the Ron Williamson story has happened over and over. Since 1976, Illinois has executed 12 people—and freed 13 from death row as innocent. Last week Illinois Gov. George Ryan declared a *moratorium* on executions. The next day a California judge threw out the convictions of nine people after prosecutors said they were among at least 32 framed by a group of corrupt police officers within the Los Angeles Police Department. New innocence cases, based on DNA tests, are on the horizon in California, Texas, Florida and Louisiana.

A rare moment of enlightenment is at hand. In the last decade, DNA tests have provided stone-cold proof that 69 people were sent to prison and death row in North America for crimes they did not commit. The number has been rising at a rate of more than one a month. What matters most is not how the wrongly convicted got out of jail, but how they got into it. "How do you prevent another innocent man or woman from paying the ultimate penalty for a crime he or she did not commit?" asked Governor Ryan, a Republican and death-penalty supporter. "Today I cannot answer that question."

In 22 states, the fabric of false guilt has been laid bare, and the same vivid threads bind a wealthy Oklahoma businessman and a Maryland fisherman; a Marine corporal in California and a boiler repairman in Virginia; a Chicago drifter and a Louisiana construction worker; a Missouri schoolteacher and the Oklahoma ballplayer. Sometimes, it turns out, eyewitnesses make mistakes. Snitches tell lies. Confessions are *coerced* or fabricated. Racism trumps the truth. Lab tests are rigged. Defense lawyers sleep. Cops lie.

DNA testing can't solve these problems, but it reveals their existence. Many can be fixed with simple reforms. To simply ignore them means that more criminals go free, and the innocent will suffer. Clyde Charles learned the crushing weight of the *status quo:* he was freed just before Christmas, after 19 years of his life were *squandered* in Louisiana's Angola prison. The last nine years were spent fighting for the DNA lab work that cleared him in a matter of hours. In 48 states, prisoners don't have *statutory* rights to tests that could prove their innocence, and too often authorities stubbornly resist. In more than half its *exonerations,* the Innocence Project was forced into fierce *litigation* simply to get the DNA tests.

"Our procedure," wrote Justice Learned Hand in 1923, "has always been haunted by the ghost of the innocent man convicted. It is an unreal dream." Nearly 75 years later, Judge Seay in Oklahoma wrote an *epilogue* to the writ of habeas corpus for Ron Williamson: "God help us, if ever in this great country we turn our heads while people who have not had fair trials are executed. That almost happened in this case." For all the gigabytes of crime statistics kept in the United States, no account is taken of the innocent person, wrongly convicted, ultimately *exonerated.* No one has the job of figuring out what went wrong, or who did wrong. The moment has come to do so. ■

Comprehension Quick-Check

After reading "When Justice Lets Us Down," ask your instructor for a copy of the Comprehension Quick-Check Quiz.

Building Blocks Revisited

You can use a variety of generative strategies to master the 17 targeted words in Reading B. In addition to creating vocabulary cards, you might wish to group words that have something in common. For example, *litigation, moratorium, ratified,* and *statutory* could be grouped together because they pertain to the law or legal concerns. Can you see any other groupings? Note that the word *stay* is a multiple-meaning word, so you will need to select the dictionary definition that is a noun and fits the context. After you create your vocabulary strategies for these words, complete the three Vocabulary Activities.

Vocabulary Activities

 Figuring It Out

B.1 DIRECTIONS: Answer the following questions about the 17 targeted words from Reading B.

1. What verb with a negative connotation means "to spend extravagantly or to waste"?

   _____

2. What adjective means "authorized by laws or rules made by a state or court"?

   _____

3. What noun means "a short addition or concluding section at the end of some work"?

   _____

4. What adjective means the opposite of "real or authentic"?

   _____

5. What noun means "a lawsuit"?

   _____

6. What adjective with a negative connotation means "lacking in skill or judgment"?

   _____

7. What adjective means "causing death or extremely harmful"?

_____

8. What multiple-meaning word means "a brief suspension or postponement of a legal action or execution"?

_____

9. What expression taken from Latin means "the existing or present state of affairs"?

_____

10. What verb means "to wrap or pad in order to deafen or reduce in volume"?

_____

11. What noun means "a suspension of action"?

_____

12. What adverb means "in a disorderly, rapid, and nervous way"?

_____

13. What verb means "brought about through force, threats, or pressure"?

_____

14. What noun means "a statement uttered out loud over and over again"?

_____

15. What noun means "complete disorder or ruin"?

_____

16. What verb means "approved and made sound and valid"?

_____

17. What verb means "freed from blame or responsibility"?

_____

Practicing It

B.2 DIRECTIONS: Complete the following sentences, being as specific as possible in order to demonstrate your understanding of the boldfaced words.

1. The bank teller examined the *bogus* check and decided to _____ _____ .

2. The governor decided to issue a *stay* in all executions because _____ _____ .

3. The sick child was *coerced* into taking the medicine because _____ _____ .

4. The lawyer claimed his client's *statutory* rights were violated when the policeman _____ _____ .

5. Most elderly people prefer the *status quo* because _____ _____ .

6. When a movie tells a story about a real person, the director might offer an *epilogue* because _____ _____ .

7. After the lottery winner *squandered* all his money on cars and clothes, he decided _____ _____ .

8. A community can be left in *shambles* when _____ _____ .

9. When the student heard he was *exonerated* from the charge of cheating,

   _____ .

10. Some students behave *frantically* during final exams because _____

    _____ .

11. When the parents learned that their child had been operated on by an *inept*

    doctor, they _____

    _____ .

12. Once a bill is *ratified* by a governor or a state court, _____

    _____ .

13. During the wedding, the parents were asked to *muffle* their baby's crying

    because _____

    _____ .

14. After the writing instructor issued a *moratorium* on papers, _____

    _____ .

15. After drinking a *lethal* amount of alcohol, _____

    _____ .

16. The insurance company reviewed the *litigation* on the car accident and

    _____ .

17. The college-bound senior listened to his parent's *litany* on studying and

    decided _____

    _____ .

Applying It

B.3 DIRECTIONS: Complete the following analogies using the targeted words listed below. Remember to keep the same part of speech across the analogy.

moratorium lethal bogus ratify litany epilogue status quo stay

1. authentic : _____ :: competent, skilled : inept

2. beneficial : _____ :: organized and calm : frantic

3. a suspension of action : _____ :: complete disorder or ruin : shambles

4. a conclusion or summary : _____ :: lawsuit : litigation

5. to approve : _____ :: to reduce or deafen : muffle

B.4 DIRECTIONS: Answer the following questions, making sure to provide enough detail to demonstrate your understanding of the boldfaced words.

6. Would most people have to be *coerced* into listening to a political *litany*? Why or why not?

   _____

   _____

   _____

7. If a governor issued a *stay* in a convicted killer's execution, would that individual be *exonerated*? Why or why not?

   _____

   _____

   _____

8. Can a *moratorium* on taxes be issued without a *statutory* decision? Why or why not?

   _____

   _____

   _____

9. Do individuals who frequently *squander* their paychecks in one shopping spree care about the future or the *status quo*?

_____

_____

_____

READING C

Did you know that some companies not only prohibit smoking in the workplace but also demand that employees not smoke off the job as well? Does this new hiring rule seem fair? More importantly, do you know why companies are creating these policies and rules? You will discover the background and rationale for these policies when you read "If You Light Up on Sunday, Don't Come in on Monday." Before reading the article and completing the Vocabulary Activities, evaluate your present understanding of each of the 19 targeted words. Circle 1, 2, or 3 to indicate how familiar you are with each word (see page 4 for an explanation of the rating system).

Level of Understanding

banning	1	2	3
communicable	1	2	3
deem	1	2	3
disincentives	1	2	3
estimates (verb)	1	2	3
fraternizing	1	2	3
grim	1	2	3
incentives	1	2	3
incidence	1	2	3
justifiable	1	2	3
levied	1	2	3
moonlighting	1	2	3
perk (noun)	1	2	3
proffer	1	2	3

prohibits	1	2	3
proponents	1	2	3
sentiment	1	2	3
spurred	1	2	3
surcharge	1	2	3

If You Light Up on Sunday, Don't Come in on Monday

by Zachary Schiller, Walescia Konrad, and Stephanie Anderson Forest

Two years ago, Ford Meter Box in Wabash, Ind., decided it would no longer hire any smokers. Janice Bone was a payroll clerk for the small manufacturer. When a urine test uncovered nicotine traces in Bone's sample, Ford fired her. The incident helped privacy **proponents** *pass an Indiana state law protecting employees who smoke away from work. But Bone, who has filed suit against Ford, has not gotten her job back. . . .*

Do you smoke? Drink? Eat more than you should? Your employer is getting very interested in your answer. It may cost you more in insurance coverage; there's even an off chance that it could cost you your job. As medical expenses whirl skyward, more companies have begun to see smokers, drinkers, and workers who engage in other "high-risk"—but legal—activities as a burden. Johnson & Johnson Health Management Inc. of New Brunswick, N.J., which sells wellness programs to companies, **estimates** that 15% to 25% of corporate health care costs stem from employees' "unhealthy lifestyle conditions." With health care costs rising a **grim** 9% each year, employers note, why shouldn't individual employees take responsibility for their behavior—especially since corporate health coverage is a **perk** in the first place?

The employers' concerns are **justifiable.** Still, they raise a range of questions about the employee's right to privacy away from the workplace. So far, only a handful of companies have taken the extreme stand of Ford Meter . . . [b]ut many others are instituting **disincentives** for staffers they **deem** high-risk—charging them more for health insurance, for example.

Existing civil rights laws don't generally protect against "lifestyle discrimination," because smokers and skydivers aren't named as protected classes. But since 1989, 20 states have passed laws **banning** discrimination against smokers, and a few give much broader protection. The backers of such laws are tapping a wellspring of **sentiment** that employers have no business telling employees how to run their private lives, as long as what they do doesn't interfere with how they do their jobs. "When they start telling you you can't smoke on your own time, the next thing you know they'll tell you you can't have sex but once a week, and if you have sex twice a week, you're fired," declares Oklahoma State Senator Carl Franklin, a backer of Oklahoma's smoker-protection law.

AFTER HOURS. Employers have always had concerns about some off-hours activities: **moonlighting,** politicking, **fraternizing** with competitors' employees. But the technological advances and social ills of the 1980s brought with them a host of workplace privacy issues. The result was a new generation of laws and court decisions spelling out how far an employer can go in certain areas. Congress has largely banned the use of polygraph testing. The U.S. Supreme Court has upheld a federal law that **prohibits** discrimination by federal contractors against persons with **communicable** diseases such as AIDS. Ten states have restricted drug testing. . . .

SMOKE-BUSTERS. Already, many employers won't hire smokers. Since 1987, USG Corp., a Chicago building-materials maker, has banned smokers from the ranks of 1,200 workers in eight plants. Its concern: Smoking might lead to a higher **incidence** of lung disease among workers who work with mineral fiber used in making tile. Turner Broadcasting System Inc. won't hire smokers at all. "We think we have the right to employ the kind of person we want to have—and that's a non-smoker," says William M. Shaw, vice-president for administration. . . .

Cracking down on smokers is understandable, because the dangers of tobacco are so well established. The fear, of course, is that once employers start questioning one type of employee behavior, the list of unsuitable habits will grow. "Why would an employer tell you to knock off smoking at home and not tell you to knock off the beer, if the beer is bad for you, too?" asks Lewis L. Maltby, director of the American Civil Liberties Union National Task Force on Civil Liberties in the Work Place. . . .

Many companies take a positive approach, in the shape of financial **incentives** that give employees who live right the chance to profit by it. Half of the 22,000 persons covered by Southern California Edison Co.'s medical plan have reduced their annual premium by $120 under the corporation's good-health rebate program. They qualify if their weight, cholesterol, and other statistics are within certain bounds. . . .

SIN SURCHARGE. But while some companies **proffer** a carrot, others favor the stick. In a recent Harris Poll for Metropolitan Life Insurance Co., 86% of 1,175 executives surveyed found it "acceptable" to charge higher premiums for unhealthy habits. Since the presence of smokers in a work force drives the group rate up, there is a growing interest in charging smokers more for their insurance—rather than spreading the cost equally among all employees. "Why should we continue to do that when all the medical evidence says smoking leads to health problems?" asks Miller of Monsanto, which is toying with a **surcharge**.

No reason at all, or so Texas Instruments Inc. figured. **Spurred** by an in-house study showing that smokers' health costs at TI were 50% higher than non-smokers', the company began charging employees $10 a month for smoking outside work. The same sum is **levied** for up to two of the employees' dependents if they smoke, too.

The new charges have prompted no great outcry, perhaps because smokers recognize their puffing is so unpopular. Most of them are bothered, though, that the charge doesn't apply to other habits. "I think they should go and investigate all types of lifestyles that may increase risk to the company," says a TI programmer who pays $20 more each month because he and his wife smoke. "Someone who jumps out of airplanes for jollies or who races cars on weekends, that could cost the company, too." . . . ■

Comprehension Quick-Check

After reading "If You Light Up on Sunday, Don't Come in on Monday," ask your instructor for a copy of the Comprehension Quick-Check Quiz.

Building Blocks Revisited

You can use a variety of generative vocabulary strategies to learn the 19 targeted words in Reading C. Although you may have a Stage 3 understanding of some of the words, make sure to take the time to select the appropriate dictionary definition. For example, because the word **perk** is both a noun and a verb, you will need to read the dictionary entry carefully and match the definitions to the context in the article. You also should pay attention to the etymological information in each dictionary entry. And notice that the words **proffer, disincentives, prohibits,** and **surcharge** contain important word elements that should help you to remember what they mean. After you have completed your vocabulary cards and read Reading C, complete the Vocabulary Activities.

Vocabulary Activities

 Figuring It Out

C.1 DIRECTIONS: Circle the correct definition of each boldfaced word.

1. "The incident helped privacy *proponents* pass an Indiana state law protecting employees who smoke away from work."
   a. people who are against something
   b. people who go on trial for a crime
   c. people who are in favor of something
   d. people who want to smoke on the job

2. "Johnson & Johnson Health Management Inc. of New Brunswick, N.J., ... *estimates* that 15% to 25% of corporate health care costs stem from employees' 'unhealthy lifestyle conditions.'"
   a. calculates approximately
   b. wildly guesses
   c. averages
   d. believes

3. "With health care costs rising a *grim* 9% each year, ... why shouldn't individual employees take responsibility for their behavior—especially since corporate health coverage is a *perk* in the first place?" *Grim* means
   a. acceptable
   b. expected
   c. depressing
   d. average

4. *Perk* (see sentence 3) means
   a. benefit
   b. requirement
   c. law
   d. disadvantage

5. "The employers' concerns are *justifiable*."
   a. unfounded
   b. incorrect
   c. proven
   d. shown to be valid

6. "So far, only a handful of companies have taken the extreme stance of Ford Meter ... [b]ut many others are instituting *disincentives* for staffers they *deem* high-risk—charging them more for health insurance, for example." *Disincentives* means
   a. advantages
   b. problems
   c. penalties
   d. gifts

7. *Deem* (see sentence 6) means
   a. misinterpret
   b. suspect
   c. praise
   d. judge

8. "But since 1989, 20 states have passed laws *banning* discrimination against smokers . . ."
   a. promoting
   b. suggesting
   c. legalizing
   d. prohibiting

9. "The backers of such laws are tapping a wellspring of *sentiment* that employers have no business telling employees how to run their private lives . . ."
   a. beliefs
   b. prejudices
   c. issues
   d. comments

10. "Employers have always had concerns about some off-hours activities: *moonlighting*, politicking, *fraternizing* with competitors' employees." *Moonlighting* means
    a. working the night shift
    b. working a second job
    c. working for a competitor
    d. being unemployed

11. *Fraternizing* (see sentence 10) means
    a. associating with others
    b. making others angry with you
    c. outdoing others
    d. spying on others

12. "The U.S. Supreme Court has upheld a federal law that *prohibits* discrimination by federal contractors against persons with *communicable* diseases . . ." *Prohibits* means
    a. allows
    b. demands
    c. permits
    d. forbids

13. *Communicable* (see sentence 12) means something
    a. deadly
    b. catchable from another person
    c. curable
    d. not curable

14. "Smoking might lead to a higher *incidence* of lung disease among workers . . ."
    a. ratio
    b. cause
    c. promotion
    d. occurrence

15. "Many companies take a positive approach, in the shape of financial *incentives* . . ."
    a. benefits
    b. penalties
    c. problems
    d. punishments

16. "But while some companies *proffer* a carrot, others favor the stick."
    a. donate
    b. take back
    c. give
    d. oppose

17. "'Why should we continue to do that when all medical evidence says smoking leads to health problems?' asks Miller of Monsanto, which is toying with a *surcharge*."
    a. incentive
    b. surplus
    c. additional charge
    d. refund

18. "*Spurred* by an in-house study showing that smokers' health costs at TI were 50% higher than nonsmokers' . . ."
    a. urged on
    b. held back
    c. discouraged
    d. supplemented

19. "The sum is *levied* for up to two of the employees' dependents if they smoke, too."
    a. collected
    b. refunded
    c. deposited
    d. enforced

Practicing It

C.2 DIRECTIONS: Fill in the blanks with words from the list of targeted words in Reading C. Each word is used only once.

1. The jury's decision to convict the accused criminal of murder was

    _____ , based on the large amount of evidence presented by

    the prosecution.

2. The _____ of the bill before Congress to improve health

    care firmly believed that enough federal money was available to fund the bill.

3. The _____ of smoking on all domestic airplane flights was

    greeted with praise from flyers who are allergic to cigarette smoke.

4. Once a tax is _____ , getting it removed is difficult.

5. In the 1970s, when oil was in low supply but demand was high, many

    energy companies put a _____ on the fuel people used in

    their homes, making their bills even higher.

6. At one time the statistics on the number of people who died of smallpox

    were _____ , but with the help of vaccinations, there are

    hardly any cases anywhere in the world currently.

7–8. In day care centers, there is a high _____ of _____ diseases because sick children are rarely kept home, and at the centers they generally are in close contact with others.

9. Samuel was working as a bank teller during the day but was _____ as a bartender four nights a week to help pay off his college loans.

10. County or city law often _____ pet owners from letting their dogs roam freely in their neighborhoods.

11. In order to figure out your insurance premiums, a company _____ how likely you are to have an accident, based on your past driving record.

12. Many small business owners believe that providing health insurance to their employees is a _____ , not a right.

13. Before her death, it was Lauren's _____ that she be cremated.

14. _____ to doing well in college might include landing a high-paying job or getting into graduate school.

15. Things that you _____ to be important will be the things that you give great care and attention to.

16. Because Harley was caught _____ with nonunion workers, he almost lost his job and many friends.

17. When you _____ your opinion, you should be willing to accept the fact that others might disagree with you.

18. Among the _____ to smoking would be payment of higher insurance premiums.

19. _____ on by the hoots and hollers of the crowd, the band

played another set, which turned out to be their best of the night.

 Applying It

C.3 **DIRECTIONS:** For each of the following items, give an example
that demonstrates your understanding of the boldfaced word.

1. A job you might have if you were *moonlighting* _____

_____

2–3. An *incidence* requiring you to pay a *surcharge* _____

_____

4–5. Something that has been *prohibited* or *banned* _____

_____

6. Something that you *deem* to be important to success _____

_____

7. A disease that has *grim* consequences _____

_____

8–9. A time when it might be *justifiable* to *levy* new taxes _____

_____

10. A time when your *sentiments* differed from everyone else's _____

_____

11. A disease that is *communicable* _____

_____

12. A *perk* you might receive if you worked for an important movie producer

_____

_____

13. An instance when *fraternizing* with your coworkers may do you more

harm than good _____

_____

14–15. An *incentive* and a *disincentive* for going to the doctor _____

_____

16. What an animal rights *proponent* might say at a rally _____

_____

17. Something that the federal government *estimates* every year _____

_____

18. An instance when a strong belief *spurred* you into action _____

_____

19. A situation in which you did not want to *proffer* your thoughts about some-

thing _____

_____

▶ Extending

DIRECTIONS: Several of the targeted words in Chapter 5 have suffixes. Look at each of the word pairs below, and think about what happens to the bold-faced words when a suffix is added or changed. In some cases the part of speech may not change, but the suffix changes the meaning of the word. You may need to use your vocabulary cards and the dictionary to fill in the blanks correctly.

1. *fraternizing*

   Part of speech: _____

   Meaning: _____

   fraternity

   Part of speech: _____

   Meaning: _____

   Sentence for *fraternity:* _____

2. *justifiable*

   Part of speech: _____

   Meaning: _____

   justify

   Part of speech: _____

   Meaning: _____

   Sentence for *justify:* _____

3. *consolation*

   Part of speech: _____

   Meaning: _____

   console

   Part of speech: _____

   Meaning: _____

   Sentence for *console:* _____

4. *distinctions*

Part of speech: _____

Meaning: _____

distinct

Part of speech: _____

Meaning: _____

Sentence for *distinct:* _____

Evaluating

Review and test yourself on the 49 targeted words in this chapter. Then ask your instructor for the comprehensive exam on these words.

6 Practice 2

DID YOU KNOW?

The word *berserk* originated from Norse mythology. Berserk was a fierce man who used no armor and assumed the form of a wild beast in battle. Supposedly, no enemy could touch him. Today, if you are described as *berserk*, you are wild, dangerous, and crazed.

READING A

Reading A, "In Praise of the F Word," presents one person's opinion on *flunking* students—the *F word* in this case. The author suggests that awarding high school diplomas to students who are semiliterate does a disservice to everyone—the school, the student, and the future employer. Think for a minute about your own high school experience. Do you know of students who graduated but could barely read? Do you think they should have flunked until they mastered the information demanded by the curriculum? Before reading the article and completing the Vocabulary Activities, evaluate your present understanding of each of the 14 targeted words. Circle 1, 2, or 3 to indicate how familiar you are with each word (see page 4 for an explanation of the rating system).

Level of Understanding

abusive	1	2	3
composure	1	2	3
conspiracy	1	2	3
dooms	1	2	3
equivalency	1	2	3

flustered	1	2	3
impediments	1	2	3
perceive	1	2	3
priority	1	2	3
radical	1	2	3
reality	1	2	3
resentful	1	2	3
semiliterate	1	2	3
validity	1	2	3

In Praise of the F Word   *by Mary Sherry*

Tens of thousands of 18-year-olds will graduate this year and be handed meaningless diplomas. These diplomas won't look any different from those awarded their luckier classmates. Their **validity** will be questioned only when their employers discover that these graduates are **semiliterate.**

Eventually a fortunate few will find their way into educational-repair shops—adult-literacy programs, such as the one where I teach basic grammar and writing. There, high-school graduates and high-school dropouts pursuing graduate-**equivalency** certificates will learn the skills they should have learned in school. They will also discover they have been cheated by our educational system.

As I teach, I learn a lot about our schools. Early in each session I ask my students to write about an unpleasant experience they had in school. No writers' block here! "I wish someone would have had made me stop doing drugs and made me study." "I liked to party and no one seemed to care." "I was a good kid and didn't cause any trouble, so they just passed me along even though I didn't read well and couldn't write." And so on.

I am your basic do-gooder, and prior to teaching this class I blamed the poor academic skills our kids have today on drugs, divorce and other **impediments** to concentration necessary for doing well in school. But, as I rediscover each time I walk into the classroom, before a teacher can expect students to concentrate, he has to get their attention, no matter what distractions may be at hand. There are many ways to do this, and they have much to do with teaching style. However, if style alone won't do it, there is another way to show who holds the winning hand in the classroom. That is to reveal the trump card of failure.

I will never forget a teacher who played that card to get the attention of one of my children. Our youngest, a world-class charmer, did little to develop his intellectual talents but always got by. Until Mrs. Stifter.

Our son was a high-school senior when he had her for English. "He sits in the back of the room talking to his friends," she told me. "Why don't you move him to the front row?" I urged, believing the embarrassment would get him to settle down. Mrs. Stifter looked at me steely-eyed over her glasses. "I don't move seniors," she said. "I flunk them." I was *flustered.* Our son's academic life flashed before my eyes. No teacher had ever threatened him with that before. I regained my *composure* and managed to say that I thought she was right. By the time I got home I was feeling pretty good about this. It was a *radical* approach for these times, but, well, why not? "She's going to flunk you," I told my son. I did not discuss it any further. Suddenly English became a *priority* in his life. He finished out the semester with an A.

I know one example doesn't make a case, but at night I see a parade of students who are angry and *resentful* for having been passed along until they could no longer even pretend to keep up. Of average intelligence or better, they eventually quit school, concluding they were too dumb to finish. "I should have been held back" is a comment I hear frequently. Even sadder are those students who are high-school graduates who say to me after a few weeks of class, "I don't know how I ever got a high-school diploma."

Passing students who have not mastered the work cheats them and the employers who expect graduates to have basic skills. We excuse this dishonest behavior by saying kids can't learn if they come from terrible environments. No one seems to stop to think that—no matter what environments they come from—most kids don't put school first on their list unless they *perceive* something is at stake. They'd rather be sailing.

Many students I see at night could give expert testimony on unemployment, chemical dependency, *abusive* relationships. In spite of these difficulties, they have decided to make education a priority. They are motivated by the desire for a better job or the need to hang on to the one they've got. They have a healthy fear of failure.

People of all ages can rise above their problems, but they need to have a reason to do so. Young people generally don't have the maturity to value education in the same way my adult students value it. But fear of failure, whether economic or academic, can motivate both.

Flunking as a regular policy has just as much merit today as it did two generations ago. We must review the threat of flunking and see it as it really is—a positive teaching tool. It is an expression of confidence by both teachers and parents that the students have the ability to learn the material presented to them. However, making it work again would take a dedicated, caring **conspiracy** between teachers and parents. It would mean facing the tough **reality** that passing kids who haven't learned the material—while it might save them grief for the short term—**dooms** them to long-term illiteracy. It would mean that teachers would have to follow through on their threats, and parents would have to stand behind them, knowing their children's best interests are indeed at stake. This means no more doing Scott's assignments for him because he might fail. No more passing Jodi because she's such a nice kid.

This is a policy that worked in the past and can work today. A wise teacher, with the support of his parents, gave our son the opportunity to succeed—or fail. It's time we return this choice to all students. ■

Comprehension Quick-Check

After reading "In Praise of the F Word," ask your instructor for a copy of the Comprehension Quick-Check Quiz.

Building Blocks Revisited

As you are completing the activities and learning the targeted words in Reading A, it is important to use the most effective and efficient generative strategies and approaches. Remember that you want to learn these words conceptually so that you can use them in your writing and in your conversations. Because several of the words contain word elements—*semiliterate, validity,* and *equivalency,* just to name three—review Chapter 4. Perhaps the words in this chapter will be easy for you to learn because you remember what the prefixes and suffixes mean.

You also might think about using imagery, which was discussed in Chapter 2, to help you learn some of the words. For instance, if you are having difficulty remembering the meaning of *composure,* you might try using this keyword and imagery strategy:

> In the word *composure* you can see the small part *posure. Posure* looks very much like the real word *posture* except that the *t* is missing. Picture yourself in a very relaxed posture—perhaps you have just finished an important exam and have nothing to do for the weekend. Maybe you are in a relaxed posture sitting on a beach or on your porch thinking about how well you have done during the week.

You are in a relaxed posture because you feel "calm and peaceful," the meaning of *composure*. You might image something that looks like this:

Draw such an image on the front of your vocabulary card. Then try to use a combination of imagery, keywords, and mnemonics to remember the rest of the targeted words. For example, what small part of a word can you see in *conspiracy*?

For the remainder of the words, vocabulary cards might be your best strategy.

Vocabulary Activities

 Figuring It Out

A.1 DIRECTIONS: Look up each boldfaced word in your dictionary. Then circle the correct definition of each one. To gain a conceptual understanding of these words and to use the definitions to help you with later activities, you may want to write the definitions on vocabulary cards, as outlined in Chapter 2. Before you make your selection, be sure to return to Reading A and see how the word is used in context.

1. "Their *validity* will be questioned . . ."
   a. practicality
   b. soundness or effectiveness
   c. humor
   d. seriousness

2. ". . . these graduates are *semiliterate.*"
   a. able to read and write at only an elementary level
   b. some of the capabilities of college students
   c. fluent in two languages
   d. late and disorganized half of the time

3. ". . . pursuing graduate-*equivalency* certificates . . ."
   a. extremely easy
   b. significantly different
   c. equal in force or value
   d. very common

4. ". . . and other *impediments* to concentration necessary for doing well in school."
   a. people who assist or help
   b. skills or attitudes that increase
   c. economic conditions that unite
   d. things that block or prevent

5. "I was *flustered.*"
   a. upset
   b. excited
   c. relieved
   d. confused

6. "I regained my *composure* . . ."
   a. concern
   b. ability to disagree
   c. calmness or peace of mind
   d. speaking voice

7. "It was a *radical* approach for these times . . ."
   a. out-of-date
   b. extreme
   c. fashionable
   d. violent

8. "Suddenly English became a *priority* in his life."
   a. fear
   b. condition of happiness
   c. burden
   d. item of importance or urgency

9. ". . . students who are angry and *resentful* . . ."
   a. quietly happy because of receiving rewards
   b. raging and violent
   c. angry because of being treated unjustly
   d. relieved and accepting

10. ". . . unless they *perceive* something is at stake."
    a. understand
    b. demand
    c. ask
    d. cooperate

11. ". . . could give expert testimony on unemployment, chemical dependency, *abusive* relationships."
    a. strong, lasting
    b. sexual
    c. hurtful, injurious
    d. meaningful

12. ". . . would take a dedicated, caring *conspiracy* between teachers and parents."
    a. situation
    b. discussion
    c. strong disagreement over issues
    d. secret plan or plot for a bold purpose

13. "It would mean facing the tough *reality* . . ."
    a. frightening situation
    b. actual or true situation
    c. severe or strict rules
    d. final event

14. "... ***dooms*** them to long-term illiteracy."
    a. condemns
    b. criticizes
    c. prevents
    d. insults

A.2 DIRECTIONS: As mentioned in Chapter 4, word elements can sometimes be useful in determining or recalling the meaning of a word. Several of the 14 targeted words in Reading A have interesting prefixes. Using your knowledge of word elements and a dictionary, supply the appropriate words.

15. Which word begins with a prefix meaning "half"?

    _____

16. What other words do you know that begin with that prefix? Check a dictionary for two examples of words that are new to you. Write each below, and provide a definition of each.

    a. _____

    b. _____

17. Which word begins with a prefix that means "to be just or equal in value"?

    _____

18. What other words do you know that begin with that prefix? Check a dictionary for two examples of words that are new to you. Write each below, and provide a definition of each.

    a. _____

    b. _____

Practicing It

A.3 DIRECTIONS: Complete the following sentences, being as specific as possible in order to demonstrate your understanding of the boldfaced words.

1. After hiring the *semiliterate* adult to do his payroll and bookkeeping, the

   owner _____

   _____ .

2. *Impediments* to succeeding in college include _____

   _____ .

3. The beauty pageant contestant quickly lost her *composure* when _____

   _____ .

4. Corporations and businesses place a *priority* on _____

   _____ .

5. The English professor's *abusive* comments about the freshman's paper

   _____

   _____ .

6. She thought there was a *conspiracy* between her parents to _____

   _____ .

7. The musician's *radical* ideas caused people to _____

   _____ .

8. During the game, the quarterback became so *flustered* that _____

   _____ .

9. The girl felt *resentful* toward her older sister because _____

   _____ .

10. Many people believe that the lack of a college education will *doom* you to

    _____

    _____ .

11. The bartender questioned the *validity* of _____

_____ .

12. When talking with people from other cultures, it is sometimes difficult to

perceive _____

_____ .

13. Some college freshmen wonder about the *equivalency* between _____

_____ .

14. Everyone has to face the *reality* that _____

_____ .

Applying It

A.4 DIRECTIONS: Complete the following analogies using the targeted words listed below. Remember to keep the same part of speech across the analogy. Two of the analogies test your knowledge of opposites.

radical   impediment
conspiracy   perceive
priority   equivalent

1. extreme : _____ :: harmful : abusive

2. unequal : _____ :: calm : flustered

3. to misunderstand : to _____ :: to glorify : to doom

4. obstruction : _____ :: peacefulness : composure

A.5 DIRECTIONS: When you can provide an example of a word, you generally have a good conceptual understanding of that word. Follow the instructions below, and if necessary explain your choices. Be sure to demonstrate your knowledge of the boldfaced words.

5. Give an example of a ***conspiracy*** that you or someone you know has experienced. Explain why it would qualify as a ***conspiracy.*** _____

_____

6. What items that you possess or own should be ***valid*** (adjective form of the noun ***validity***)? Why is this ***validity*** critical? _____

_____

7. What daily tasks would a ***semiliterate*** individual find difficult? (Be specific.)

_____

_____

8. Give two examples of ***priorities*** in your life. Why have you ***prioritized*** (verb form of ***priority***) them? _____

_____

9. When have you or someone you know been ***resentful***? What caused this ***resentment*** (noun form of ***resentful***)? _____

_____

10. When have you lost your ***composure***? What caused this loss of ***composure***?

_____

_____

11. As you grow older, you learn to face ***realities.*** List one unpleasant and one pleasant ***reality*** that you have faced or will face. _____

_____

READING B

Reading B, "Confessions of a Former Chauvinist Pig," allows us to examine how a now-middle-aged man lived through, and came to grips with, what has been called the sexual revolution. You probably don't remember the time when a woman's "job" was to have and care for children and do housework, not to work outside the home. Women were considered the "fairer sex," and men and women were believed to differ from one another in many ways. Writer David Bouchier remembers what things used to be like and contrasts then with now. As you read this selection, think about whether you agree with Bouchier. Were your home life and family similar to his or different? Have you experienced any of the situations he discusses? What is your view of the role of women in today's society? Before reading the article and completing the Vocabulary Activities, evaluate your present understanding of each of the 19 targeted words. Circle 1, 2, or 3 to indicate how familiar you are with each word (see page 4 for an explanation of the rating system).

Level of Understanding

abolition	1	2	3
androgyny	1	2	3
baffled	1	2	3
chauvinism	1	2	3
déjà vu	1	2	3
deviousness	1	2	3
domestic	1	2	3
egalitarian	1	2	3
entrepreneur	1	2	3
indicted	1	2	3
intriguing	1	2	3
jargon	1	2	3
liberation	1	2	3
nostalgic	1	2	3
oppressed	1	2	3
passive	1	2	3
proposition	1	2	3

| provisional | 1 | 2 | 3 |
| tedious | 1 | 2 | 3 |

Confessions of a Former Chauvinist Pig   *by David Bouchier*

Young men today take their ***egalitarian*** relationships with women for granted. They think it was *always* OK for men to express their feelings, change diapers and go all the way on a first date. Nobody remembers the casualties, the men who went to the wall for equality when the wall was a million miles high.

We male veterans of the sex war are past middle age now, and still repent of our past sins and present failings. Raised in ***chauvinism, indicted*** by feminism and bypassed by the sexual revolution, some of us have spent half our lives coming to terms with the slippery idea of women's equality.

Most men were stunned when a militant feminist movement appeared in the late '60s. It had never occurred to us that women were ***oppressed.*** They seemed to do extraordinarily well, sexually and economically, out of the games we all played. After all, who was setting the rules?

The rules of courtship, for example—the chaste dates, the first kiss, the gifts, the first meeting with her parents—were things that young men had to learn the way rats learn their way through laboratory mazes. The game made no sense to us, but we ran the maze out of training and habit.

Having played the game, we collected the prize—marriage and suburban life. About three days later, or so it seemed, along came feminism and the sexual revolution. All the rules changed. Women were declared the equals of men, and no longer to be treated as ***passive*** wives and sex objects. The New Woman would be sexually and economically free, just like a man.

"I wouldn't mind being a sex object for just one day," muttered a confused male friend of mine, almost weeping into his beer.

But there was something ***intriguing*** about the prospect of sexual equality at last. A few men, myself included, decided that the liberation of women and the ***liberation*** of men were part of the same problem. We came to see sexual liberation as a total, revolutionary thing, one that would abolish male responsibility for women and children and equalize the sexual game. So we set out to remake our lives in the feminist mold.

Our first surprise was the discovery that sexual equality, in the ordinary, everyday sense, was a terrible bore. Women had always complained that housework and child care were ***tedious*** and exhausting. Now we knew the truth of it. The men who

"Confessions of a Former Chauvinist Pig," by David Bouchier, *Atlanta Journal and Constitution,* March 18, 1990. Reprinted by permission of David Bouchier.

took on an equal share of domestic work discovered that they had bought into a zero-sum *proposition*—one less boring job for her was one more boring job for him. Large chunks of our free time vanished into *domestic* tedium, and we got little in exchange but the cold comfort of self-righteousness.

"I'm doing the right thing," I would boast to my friends; but in my heart I knew they would be hanging out in a bar while I was cooking, or watching the game while I was shopping.

Things weren't much better at work. The flood of highly qualified women into every business and profession simply made life tougher for men, as more people competed for the same number of jobs and promotions. The war between the sexes expanded out of the home and into the office.

And, of course, the family changed. The family is our storehouse of dreams, but the new, two-career egalitarian family felt different, more businesslike, less homelike than the families we grew up in. Exit those *nostalgic* family stories of grandma the apple pie wizard and grandpa the successful *entrepreneur*. Welcome to the new post-feminist nostalgia: how grandma became a mid-level IBM executive with the support of grandpa, the busy househusband. It was all a bit depressing.

But the *abolition* of the traditional family was nothing compared to the abolition of sex. We early male enthusiasts for feminism had misunderstood the sexual consequences of equality. Sex was never about equality but about *difference*, and sexual equality implied the phasing-out of male–female differences—in the *jargon* of the times, *androgyny.*

Yet the appearance of women as different and beautiful and sexually exciting turned out to be more fundamental than we had imagined. Women who looked and acted like men *baffled* the impulse to desire and to love. Superwoman, with her business suit and busy schedule and stuffed briefcase, was simply unattractive—too much like the guy at the next desk. And Superwomen soon began to say out loud that the domesticated, emotional male was pretty unattractive too; the term "wimp" was freely used.

Many men of my generation tasted the sour grapes of equality and gave up. But some of us kept working at it. In the long run, we made some big gains, but not the ones we expected. We didn't get real sexual equality, but we did escape the breadwinner trap, and all the guilt and anxiety that went with it. We really did build better partnerships with our wives, who became more interesting as they moved out of the house and into the world. We did learn a lot about ourselves as men, most of it bad.

The struggle with the Old Adam continues. Male chauvinists, like recovering alcoholics, are never completely cured. I've been trying to make myself over into an egalitarian male for almost a quarter century. On good days, I can proclaim (to myself) a *provisional* victory. I am lucky to have a truly egalitarian marriage, and

I've learned to like and trust and admire women for their personalities and accomplishments, not just for their looks. On good days, I can feel that the feminist revolution is over and that both sexes won.

Yet so many of my friends have slipped or crawled back into traditional marriages, and the younger generation looks strangely familiar. Teaching and talking to teenagers, I get a dizzying sense of *déjà vu,* as though peering down a long funnel into the '50s.

There they are, lined up in the college classroom—row after row of Barbies and Kens. The gulf of misunderstanding between these young women and men seems as great as it was 30 years ago, and they still play the games I remember so well. Women still accuse men of coldness and faithlessness. Men still accuse women of *deviousness* and emotionality. Men still pursue, women still look away with giggles and secret smiles.

What keeps me awake some nights is this: Suppose I have finally changed, and everyone else has remained the same? ■

Comprehension Quick-Check

After reading "Confessions of a Former Chauvinist Pig," ask your instructor for a copy of the Comprehension Quick-Check Quiz.

Building Blocks Revisited

Reading B will enable you to practice your vocabulary skills in a variety of ways. Vocabulary cards will work for some words. Organizational strategies will help with others, word elements with still others. Even the keyword method may help you learn the meaning of difficult words. For example, if you have problems remembering the word *androgyny* (being both female and male in appearance), you might think about it in the following way:

> In the word *androgyny* you can see the letters *drog*. Imagine that a *drog* is a rare breed of dog that looks both male and female and no one, not even the vet, can say for certain which it is!

You could put this keyword strategy on the front of your vocabulary card.

Something else that you might notice as you go through the list of targeted words from Reading B and read the article is that many English words come from the French language. Several words in this selection either are directly taken from French or indirectly owe their existence to the French language.

Vocabulary Activities

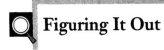

Figuring It Out

B.1 DIRECTIONS: From the list of targeted words in Reading B, select the word that best answers each question.

1. Which noun refers to the prejudiced belief that one group is superior to another group?

   _____

2. Which adjective describes household tasks such as ironing, cleaning the bathroom, and washing windows?

   _____

3. Imagine that you see someone whose appearance and behavior do not give you a clue about his or her sex. Which noun refers to this condition?

   _____

4. Which adjective describes a homework assignment that is uninteresting and tiresome?

   _____

5. Which adjective describes an individual who is not active and prefers to do nothing?

   _____

6. What is another term for the feeling or illusion that you previously experienced some situation?

   _____

7. Which noun refers to an individual who likes to organize, operate, and assume the risks of a business?

   _____

8. Which adjective describes an individual who feels frustrated or blocked at some job or task?

   _____

9. Which noun refers to the act of completely ending or getting rid of something?

   _____

10. Which noun refers to the condition of being shifty, tricky, and dishonest?

    _____

11. Which adjective describes a situation that is satisfactory for the time being but eventually will change with some permanent arrangement?

    _____

12. Which adjective describes the belief or doctrine that equal rights for all individuals are a must?

    _____

13. Which noun means "plan or statement"?

    _____

14. Which noun refers to specialized language or talk of a particular trade, such as might be used by baseball players or computer specialists?

    _____

15. Which adjective describes a situation that might arouse your curiosity or interest?

    _____

16. Which noun refers to the action of trying to free a group from confinement and control by another group?

    _____

17. Which adjective describes the feelings you have when you long or desire for the things, persons, or situations of your past?

_____

18. Which verb means "accused of wrongdoing"?

_____

19. Which adjective describes a group that might feel overwhelmed or crushed and bothered unjustly through the use of force or an authority?

_____

Practicing It

B.2 DIRECTIONS: Complete the following sentences, being as specific as possible in order to demonstrate your understanding of the boldfaced words.

1. A *baffled* student in a math class might _____

_____ .

2. Most adults feel *nostalgic* about _____

_____ .

3. When you find someone *intriguing*, you want to _____

_____ .

4. After being assigned numerous *domestic* tasks, the adolescent _____

_____ .

5. Her *deviousness* was obvious when she _____

_____ .

6. If you had an experience of *déjà vu,* you would _____

_____ .

7. The older man demonstrated his ***chauvinism*** when he _____

   _____ .

8. You know you have observed an example of ***androgyny*** when you _____

   _____

   _____ .

9. Because the employer granted the new employee ***provisional*** status, the

   worker _____

   _____ .

10. The group supporting ***abolition*** of the law _____

    _____ .

11. Most people try to avoid ***tedious*** jobs such as _____

    _____ .

12. When we say that the businessman offered his client a ***proposition,*** we

    mean _____

    _____ .

13. If you feel ***oppressed,*** you might _____

    _____ .

14. A ***passive*** football fan would _____

    _____ .

15. Her ***egalitarian*** attitudes and beliefs were obvious when she _____

    _____ .

16. After hearing that they would be ***indicted*** for the theft, they _____

    _____ .

17. If your psychology instructor uses a lot of *jargon*, you should _____

_____ .

18. *Entrepreneurs* are individuals who enjoy _____

_____ .

19. Groups demanding *liberation* include _____

_____ .

Applying It

B.3 DIRECTIONS: Choose the word that does not relate to the other two words. Write it in the blank after "Exclude." In the blank labeled "General concept" write a concept or idea that describes the two related words.

Example:

    funny   **a.** Exclude <u>serious</u>

    serious   **b.** General concept: <u>characteristics of comedians</u>

    humorous

1. egalitarian   **a.** Exclude _____

    liberation   **b.** General concept: _____

    chauvinism

2. tedious   **a.** Exclude _____

    intriguing   **b.** General concept: _____

    exciting

3. oppressive   **a.** Exclude _____

    devious   **b.** General concept: _____

    honest

B.4 DIRECTIONS: When you can provide an example of a word, you generally have a good conceptual understanding of that word. Follow the instructions below, and if necessary explain your choices. Be sure to demonstrate your knowledge of the boldfaced words.

4. Give an example of *androgynous* (the adjective form of *androgyny*) clothing.

_____

_____

5. Give an example of a rule that you believe should be *abolished* (verb form of *abolition*). Then explain why you believe *abolition* is necessary.

_____

_____

6. Give an example of a time when you were *baffled,* and explain why.

_____

_____

7. Give an example of a time when you experienced feelings of *déjà vu.*

_____

_____

8. Give two examples of *domestic* tasks that you do not mind doing. Explain why you find them acceptable.

_____

_____

9. Give an example of something for which someone could receive an *indictment* (noun form of *indicted*).

_____

_____

10. Give two examples of *jargon* that you use that your friends probably do not understand. From what field or area of interest do these words come?

_____

_____

11. Give an example of a *passive* behavior in the classroom.

_____

_____

12. Give an example of something that makes you or your relatives *nostalgic.*

_____

_____

13. Give an example of a *proposition* that you received at some time.

_____

_____

14. Give an example of a time when *provisional* approval would be satisfactory and an example of a time when *provisional* approval might be annoying.

_____

_____

15. Give an example of a famous *entrepreneur* who has made a fortune from his or her deals.

_____

_____

READING C

In Reading C, "The Internet and Gutenberg," Robert J. Samuelson takes an interesting perspective on the significance of the Internet and its possible legacy. He challenges the idea that the Internet "rivals the importance of Gutenberg's invention of the printing press in the 15th century," and he proposes that we suffer from "historical amnesia" when it comes to understanding the importance of inventions and movements. Think for a moment about your beliefs about the importance of the Internet. Has the Internet changed your life in any way? Can you remember a time when you went to a store to make your purchases rather than using the point-and-click method of selection? To what extent do you think the growth of the Internet has influenced the lives of your friends and family? Before reading the article and completing the Vocabulary Activities, evaluate your present understanding of each of the 23 targeted words. Circle 1, 2, or 3 to indicate how familiar you are with each word (see page 4 for an explanation of the rating system).

Level of Understanding

amnesia	1	2	3
autonomy	1	2	3
brashest	1	2	3
buffs (noun)	1	2	3
conventional	1	2	3
empowers	1	2	3
flourishes	1	2	3
fostered	1	2	3
inaugurated	1	2	3
inevitably	1	2	3
infringe	1	2	3
materialize	1	2	3
plausible	1	2	3
prosperity	1	2	3
puny	1	2	3
self-absorbed	1	2	3
speculations	1	2	3
suburbanized	1	2	3
transcendent	1	2	3
underhyped	1	2	3
undermining	1	2	3
viability	1	2	3
vindicate	1	2	3

The Internet and Gutenberg   *by Robert J. Samuelson*

In history's sweep, it may also rank behind the car, the plane and antibiotics—among others

In our *self-absorbed* age, everything is the newest New Thing or the biggest Big Thing. This spirit *inevitably* invests the Internet with *transcendent* significance. Steve Case of America Online already calls the new century "the Internet Century," and some authorities whisper that the Internet rivals the importance of Gutenberg's invention of the printing press in the 15th century. We suffer from historical *amnesia.*

Suppose you were born in 1900. You wouldn't yet watch movies (the first big silent hit, "The Great Train Robbery," showed in 1903), let alone imagine global TV. The airplane hadn't been invented, and Henry Ford wouldn't produce the first Model T until 1908. Fewer than 10 percent of U.S. homes had phones, and fewer than 8 percent had electricity. Antibiotics hadn't been discovered. As yet the Internet isn't in the same league with these developments.

Each changed lifestyles and popular beliefs. The automobile *suburbanized* America and *inaugurated* mass travel. Antibiotics, vaccines and public-health advances helped raise life expectancy from 47 in 1900 to 77 today. The explosion of *prosperity*—a consequence of electricity, other technologies and modern management—shortened working hours and expanded leisure. Movies and TV transformed popular culture.

The Internet is too young for anyone to foretell its ultimate significance—and time might *vindicate* the *brashest* prophecies. But some present claims aren't true. It is not true that no major innovation has spread so quickly. In 1990 only a handful of computer *buffs* used the Internet; by 1999 perhaps 38 percent of households were connected, reports Morgan Stanley Dean Witter. This roughly matches the adoption of the radio (which went from 0 to about 46 percent of households in the 1920s) and lags TV (which went from 9 percent of households in 1950 to 87 percent in 1960).

Of course, the Internet is a work in progress. If nothing else, the America Online–Time Warner merger is a gamble on the next generation of Internet technology. At present most home users have dial-up service through modems and old phone lines. The replacement technology is "broadband," which—through enhanced cable lines, fiber optics, satellites or better phone lines—would sharply raise transmission speeds. A fast phone modem today would allow a 10-megabyte file (equivalent to a 10- to 20-minute movie clip) to be downloaded in 24 minutes, says the Federal Communications Commission. Faster cable lines can do the same job in about a minute.

The Internet, television and the telephone will blend. This, at any rate, is the **conventional** wisdom. For AOL–Time Warner, the grand strategy is to provide both transmission services (Time Warner owns the second largest cable system) and "content" (from Internet services to films, TV programs, magazines, music—or something entirely new). Other companies harbor similar ambitions. But we don't know whether this vision, or some other, will **materialize.**

Technologies acquire historical weight by reshaping the human condition. Gutenberg's press led to mass literacy, **fostered** the Protestant Reformation (by **undermining** the clergy's theological monopoly) and, through the easy exchange of information, enabled the scientific revolution. In the 19th century railroads created a truly national American market that favored mass production and the consumer society. To join this league, the Internet must be more than e-mail or a marketing platform. If you buy a book or car on the Net, the critical part of the transaction is still the book or car. Especially in business-to-business commerce, the Internet may improve efficiency through more price competition and supplier choice. But these are changes of degree, not kind.

Thoughtful Internet enthusiasts offer **plausible speculations** about its greater meaning. "Over the past 200 years, we have built up industrial economies of mass production . . . and mass markets," says Esther Dyson, editor of Release 1.0, a newsletter. The Internet **empowers** consumers to escape mass markets; by making information so easy to dispense, it enables people to become independent producers. "The major impact is to give individuals more power over their lives," she says, while making it "tougher for governments, businesses—anyone—to operate in secrecy."

Kevin Kelly of *Wired* magazine, author of "New Rules for the New Economy," argues that the "Internet is actually being **underhyped.** Of all the people online in 10 years, only a tenth are online today." (Note: in 1999, there were 58 million worldwide connections, says Dataquest.) This could accelerate global commerce and weaken (for good or ill) national governments.

All the large issues remain unsettled. Will the Net enhance individual **autonomy**—or **infringe** on privacy? Will it increase people's economic independence—or expand corporate power (America Online–Time Warner would be no pygmy)? Before answers become clear, the Internet will have to attain economic **viability.** Though booming, it is now largely a capitalist charity. Almost everything on it is being given away or sold at a loss. Retail e-commerce is **puny.** In 1999 it amounted to less than .5 percent of U.S. consumer spending. Ditto for advertising. In 1999 Internet ads amounted to $1.8 billion out of total U.S. advertising of $215 billion, estimates Robert Coen of Universal McCann.

The great Internet fortunes arise mainly from stock speculation or building the infrastructure—supplying computers, software and fiber optics. Sooner or later, the investment must pay a return, or it will stop. Even if the Internet **flourishes,** it may remain smaller than earlier Big Things. Our historical amnesia could benefit from the words of a Tennessee farmer at a church meeting in the 1940s.

"Brothers and sisters, I want to tell you this," he said. "The greatest thing on earth is to have the love of God in your heart, and the next greatest is to have electricity in your home." Can the Internet really top that? ■

Comprehension Quick-Check

After reading "The Internet and Gutenberg," ask your instructor for a copy of the Comprehension Quick-Check Quiz.

Building Blocks Revisited

As you work through the activities related to the targeted words in Reading C, pay particular attention to the dictionary definition. Remember what we stressed about dictionary use in Chapter 3—all dictionary definitions are not equal in terms of the quality of information provided. Also remember that the dictionary definition is only one of several pieces of information that will help you learn words conceptually—it supplies mainly denotative (as opposed to connotative) meaning.

Let's look at two examples from Reading C, one word that has a strong definition and another word that has a weak definition. The definition for the word *buffs* as it is used in the reading actually has its own entry (it is not mixed in with other definitions of *buff*). The context refers to "computer *buffs*." The definition that matches this context is clear and even provides another context for the word: "One that is enthusiastic and knowledgeable about a subject: a Civil War buff." Thus it's easy to see that "computer *buffs*" would enjoy dealing with computers and have considerable knowledge about them.

On the other hand, the dictionary definition of *transcendent* is less helpful. The definition states that *transcendent* means "Surpassing others; preeminent or supreme." The context talks about the Internet having "*transcendent* significance." Although you might be able to come up with a vague idea of what *transcendent* means, the definition is certainly not as clear as that for *buffs*.

Vocabulary Activities

 ### Figuring It Out

C.1 DIRECTIONS: Fill in each blank with the appropriate targeted word from Reading C.

Targeted Word	*Definition/Part of Speech*
1. _____	based on general practice, customary (adjective)
2. _____	small, weak (adjective)
3. _____	the ability to grow or succeed (noun)
4. _____	surpassing others, supreme (adjective)
5. _____	to cause to become real or actual (verb)
6. _____	partial or total loss of memory (noun)
7. _____	gives authority to someone or some group (verb)
8. _____	consideration of a topic or idea (noun)
9. _____	most unthinking or insensitive (adjective)
10. _____	prospers, fares well (verb)
11. _____	to justify or prove worthy of, especially in light of later developments (verb)
12. _____	possible, likely (adjective)
13. _____	the condition of having success or of being well-to-do (noun)
14. _____	complete independence (noun)
15. _____	individuals who are enthusiastic and knowledgeable about a subject (noun)
16. _____	concerned only about oneself (adjective)
17. _____	to violate someone's rights, to overstep accepted limits (verb)
18. _____	caused to begin or officially started (verb)
19. _____	transformed into suburbs (verb)
20. _____	weakening by wearing away a base or foundation (noun)
21. _____	unavoidably, predictably (adverb)

Targeted Word	*Definition/Part of Speech*
22. _____	underpromoted, downplayed (adjective)
23. _____	advanced, promoted (verb)

Practicing It

C.2 D I R E C T I O N S : Read each sentence carefully. If the boldfaced word is used correctly, circle *C* and go on to the next item. If the boldfaced word is used incorrectly, circle *I* and then make the sentence correct.

C I   **1.** Health care plans rarely pay for *conventional* cancer treatments.

C I   **2.** Only the *brashest* of individuals would pick a fight with someone who is *puny*.

C I   **3.** Being terribly *self-absorbed*, Rebecca never thought that it was even remotely *plausible* that others would ignore everything she said.

C I   **4.** The company CEO *empowered* the members of his management team by *undermining* their decisions.

C I   **5.** To *flourish* and to share in their nation's *prosperity*, all Americans must learn how to *infringe* on the rights of others.

C I   **6.** Because Juan's SAT scores are extremely high, it is *inevitable* that he will be accepted into a first-rate university.

C I   **7.** A new product that is *underhyped* is likely to have record sales.

C I   **8.** *Autonomy* is rarely an issue for beginning college students.

C I   **9.** For many women, childbirth is a *transcendent* experience.

C.3 D I R E C T I O N S : Complete the following sentences, making sure to provide enough detail to demonstrate your understanding of the boldfaced words.

10. There are *speculations* that the Internet _____

_____ .

11. As a result of his *amnesia*, Carl _____

_____ .

12. People who are computer **buffs** _____

_____ .

13. Large-scale production of automobiles **fostered suburbanization** because

_____

_____ .

14. Because proof that the soon-to-be **inaugurated** candidate had accepted

bribes failed to **materialize,** the ethics committee _____

_____ .

15. When the death-row inmate's claim of innocence was finally **vindicated,**

_____

_____ .

16. The **viability** of the Internet _____

_____ .

Applying It

C . 4   D I R E C T I O N S : Answer the following questions, making sure to provide enough detail to demonstrate your understanding of the boldfaced words.

1. What would your spouse do if he or she discovered you had **amnesia?**

_____

_____

2. What would you do if someone **infringed** on your rights as a student?

_____

_____

3. How might a teacher *empower* a *puny* child? _____

_____

4. Why might people living in the country not want to see their surroundings become *suburbanized*? _____

_____

5. If your investments *flourish* and you become *prosperous,* what might you do to safeguard that *prosperity*?_____

_____

6. What does the expression "*conventional* wisdom" mean? _____

_____

7. How might you find out if *speculations* about *underhyped* stocks are *plausible*? _____

_____

8. Why might someone who is *self-absorbed* also be *autonomous*? _____

_____

_____

9. Why might a *brash* person *inevitably* lose friends? _____

_____

10. At the *inauguration* of hunting season, what might animal rights *buffs* do?

_____

_____

11. When might evidence *materialize* that would *vindicate* someone of a crime?

_____

_____

12. What might your boss do if you *__undermine__* her directives and *__transcend__*

her decisions? _____

_____

13. What might a teenager's parents do if they question the *__viability__* of their

son's plan to pay for his car insurance? _____

_____

▶ **Extending**

C.5 DIRECTIONS: Knowing the meaning of prefixes, suffixes, and roots can help you figure out the meaning of other word forms. You should be familiar with the first word in each of the following pairs because you learned it in one of the readings in this chapter. The second word, however, has been altered. Define each word, and identify its part of speech.

1. *priority*

Part of speech: _____

Definition: _____

prioritize

Part of speech: _____

Definition: _____

2. *semiliterate*

Part of speech: _____

Definition: _____

literate

Part of speech: _____

Definition: _____

3. *abolition*

   Part of speech: _____

   Definition: _____

   abolish

   Part of speech: _____

   Definition: _____

4. *chauvinism*

   Part of speech: _____

   Definition: _____

   chauvinist

   Part of speech: _____

   Definition: _____

5. *oppressed*

   Part of speech: _____

   Definition: _____

   oppressive

   Part of speech: _____

   Definition: _____

6. *prosperity*

   Part of speech: _____

   Definition: _____

   prosperous

   Part of speech: _____

   Definition: _____

7. *speculations*

   Part of speech: _____

   Definition: _____

   speculative

   Part of speech: _____

   Definition: _____

8. *viability*

   Part of speech: _____

   Definition: _____

   viable

   Part of speech: _____

   Definition: _____

Evaluating

Review and test yourself on the 56 words in this chapter. Then ask your instructor for a comprehensive exam on these words.

7

Practice 3

DID YOU KNOW?

The word *sinister* originated from an old superstition that the left side is unlucky and from the Latin word *sinister,* meaning left. Today a *sinister* person is evil.

READING A

Reading A, "A Fable for Tomorrow," is taken from the book *Silent Spring* by Rachel Carson. In this excerpt the author asks you to visualize an imaginary town. Once beautiful and alive, this town has become so polluted by humans that little life exists. Carson wants you to think about what humans do to the land and how a great deal of pollution could be avoided. Think for a minute about the place where you live. Has your local newspaper described events that are causing damage to the environment in your own hometown? What is the greatest cause of pollution? Automobiles? Industry? Landfills? Before reading the article and completing the Vocabulary Activities, evaluate your present understanding of each of the 12 targeted words. Circle 1, 2, or 3 to indicate how familiar you are with each word (see page 4 for an explanation of the rating system).

Level of Understanding

anglers	1	2	3
blight	1	2	3
brooded	1	2	3
counterparts	1	2	3
droned	1	2	3
harmony	1	2	3

maladies	1	2	3
moribund	1	2	3
prosperous	1	2	3
specter	1	2	3
stark	1	2	3
withered	1	2	3

A Fable for Tomorrow *by Rachel Carson*

There was once a town in the heart of America where all life seemed to live in **harmony** with its surroundings. The town lay in the midst of a checkerboard of **prosperous** farms, with fields of grain and hillsides of orchards where, in spring, white clouds of bloom drifted above the green fields. In autumn, oak and maple and birch set up a blaze of color that flamed and flickered across a backdrop of pines. Then foxes barked in the hills and deer silently crossed the fields, half hidden in the mists of the fall mornings.

Along the roads, laurel, viburnum and alder, great ferns and wildflowers delighted the traveler's eye through much of the year. Even in winter the roadsides were places of beauty, where countless birds came to feed on the berries and on the seed heads of the dried weeds rising above the snow. The countryside was, in fact, famous for the abundance and variety of its bird life, and when the flood of migrants was pouring through in spring and fall people traveled from great distances to observe them. Others came to fish the streams, which flowed clear and cold out of the hills and contained shady pools where trout lay. So it had been from the days many years ago when the first settlers raised their houses, sank their wells, and built their barns.

Then a strange **blight** crept over the area and everything began to change. Some evil spell had settled on the community: mysterious **maladies** swept the flocks of chickens; the cattle and sheep sickened and died. Everywhere was a shadow of death. The farmers spoke of much illness among their families. In the town the doctors had become more and more puzzled by new kinds of sickness appearing among their patients. There had been several sudden and unexplained deaths, not only among adults but even among children, who would be stricken suddenly while at play and die within a few hours.

There was a strange stillness. The birds, for example—where had they gone? Many people spoke of them, puzzled and disturbed. The feeding stations in the backyards were deserted. The few birds seen anywhere were ***moribund;*** they trembled violently and could not fly. It was a spring without voices. On the mornings that had once throbbed with the dawn chorus of robins, catbirds, doves, jays, wrens, and scores of other bird voices there was now no sound; only silence lay over the fields and woods and marsh.

On the farms the hens ***brooded,*** but no chicks hatched. The farmers complained that they were unable to raise any pigs—the litters were small and the young survived only a few days. The apple trees were coming into bloom but no bees ***droned*** among the blossoms, so there was no pollination and there would be no fruit.

The roadsides, once so attractive, were now lined with browned and ***withered*** vegetation as though swept by fire. These, too, were silent, deserted by all living things. Even the streams were now lifeless. ***Anglers*** no longer visited them, for all the fish had died.

In the gutters under the eaves and between the shingles of the roofs, a white granular powder still showed a few patches; some weeks before it had fallen like snow upon the roofs and the lawns, the fields and streams.

No witchcraft, no enemy action had silenced the rebirth of new life in this stricken world. The people had done it themselves.

This town does not actually exist, but it might easily have a thousand ***counterparts*** in America or elsewhere in the world. I know of no community that has experienced all the misfortunes I describe. Yet every one of these disasters has actually happened somewhere, and many real communities have already suffered a substantial number of them. A grim ***specter*** has crept upon us almost unnoticed, and this imagined tragedy may easily become a ***stark*** reality we all shall know.

What has already silenced the voices of spring in countless towns in America? This book is an attempt to explain. ■

Comprehension Quick-Check

After reading "A Fable for Tomorrow," ask your instructor for a copy of the Comprehension Quick-Check Quiz.

Building Blocks Revisited

Think back to what you learned in Chapter 2 about grouping together words that have something in common. This strategy will serve you well in this chapter. As you are looking up the definitions and making your vocabulary cards, look for words that have something in common. For example, a common thread links the words *withered,* *stark,* and *blight.* Can you describe that thread? Are there any other words that you could group with these three? Looking for commonalties often makes learning and remembering words easier.

In addition, you might want to use imagery to help you remember some of the words. For example, the verb *drone* means "to go on and on without stopping." As a noun, *drone* refers to a male bumblebee. Therefore, to remember *droned,* you might image on the head of a bumblebee the face of someone you consider long-winded. Your image might look something like this:

Vocabulary Activities

 Figuring It Out

A.1 DIRECTIONS: Look up each boldfaced word in your dictionary. Then circle the correct definition of each one. To gain a conceptual understanding of the word and to use the definitions to help you with later activities, you may want to write the full definition on vocabulary cards, as outlined in Chapter 2. Before you make your selection, be sure to return to the article and see how the word is used in context.

1. "...where all life seemed to live in *harmony* ..."
   a. conflict
   b. relation
   c. agreement
   d. hardship

2. "The town lay in the midst of a checkerboard of ***prosperous*** farms . . ."
   a. well-to-do
   b. small
   c. hidden
   d. useless

3. "Then a strange ***blight*** crept over the area . . ."
   a. fungus
   b. disease
   c. evil
   d. odor

4. ". . . mysterious ***maladies*** swept the flocks of chickens . . ."
   a. sicknesses
   b. deaths
   c. weather
   d. quietness

5. "The few birds seen anywhere were ***moribund*** . . ."
   a. slightly ill
   b. crippled
   c. near death
   d. without song

6. "On the farms the hens ***brooded*** . . ."
   a. pondered
   b. cackled
   c. mated
   d. sat on eggs

7. ". . . but no bees ***droned*** among the blossoms . . ."
   a. made a continuous buzzing sound
   b. flew from flower to flower
   c. made honey
   d. produced offspring

8. ". . . were now lined with browned and ***withered*** vegetation . . ."
   a. only a small amount
   b. dried up
   c. extremely hot
   d. attractive

9. "*Anglers* no longer visited them . . ."
   a. fighters
   b. traders
   c. arguers
   d. fishermen

10. ". . . it might easily have a thousand *counterparts* . . ."
    a. things with similar characteristics
    b. things with very different characteristics
    c. things that do not really exist
    d. small portions of a whole

11. "A grim *specter* has crept upon us . . ."
    a. picture
    b. plague
    c. reality
    d. threatening possibility

12. ". . . may easily become a *stark* reality . . ."
    a. naked
    b. obvious
    c. harsh
    d. unrealistic

Practicing It

A.2 DIRECTIONS: Several of the targeted words in Reading A contain roots that are fairly common. Because these roots are common, they can help you unlock the meanings of other words with which you might be unfamiliar. In this activity, we examine two roots—*mal* and *mori.*

1. The word *maladies* contains the root *mal.* Use your dictionary to find out what this root means. The root *mal* means _____

   _____

2. Find two other words in your dictionary that also contain the root *mal.* Write these words and their meanings on the lines below.

   a. _____

   b. _____

3. The word *moribund* contains the root *mori*. Use your dictionary to find out what this root means. The root *mori* means _____

_____

4. Find two other words in your dictionary that also contain the root *mori*. Write these words and their meanings on the lines below.

a. _____

b. _____

A.3 DIRECTIONS: Read each sentence carefully. If the boldfaced word is used correctly, circle *C* and go on to the next item. If the boldfaced word is used incorrectly, circle *I* and then make the sentence correct.

C   I   **1.** The *blight* that swept across Africa provided an abundance of food for the winter.

C   I   **2.** We could tell by looking at the *withered* leaves that the plant was in good shape and required very little attention.

C   I   **3.** Individuals who are *prosperous* live in small houses and drive inexpensive cars.

C   I   **4.** Young children are often plagued by various *maladies* that they pick up from their playmates.

C   I   **5.** The *anglers* went on a weekend camping trip to hunt deer.

C   I   **6.** Because Sarah had little furniture and no pictures on the walls, her new apartment looked *stark* to everyone who visited.

C   I   **7.** Every time you entered Sam's home and heard the constant yelling, you could sense the *harmony* there.

C   I   **8.** In an attempt to keep cool on hot, humid days, Bev let the air-conditioner *drone* on in her small apartment.

C   I   **9.** The puppy appeared *moribund* as he frolicked with his new owner in the yard.

C   I   **10.** A small, rural town might be considered the *counterpart* of a big city.

C   I   **11.** Before the eggs hatched, the hens *brooded* in the henhouse.

C   I   **12.** The *specter* of a destroyed environment worries many people.

Applying It

A.4 DIRECTIONS: Choose the word that does not relate to the other three words. Write it in the blank after "Exclude." In the blank labeled "General concept" write a concept or idea that describes the three related words.

1. moribund
   lively
   deathlike
   specter

   a. Exclude _____
   b. General concept: _____
   _____

2. malady
   blight
   withered
   harmony

   a. Exclude _____
   b. General concept: _____
   _____

3. rifle
   angler
   reel
   sinker

   a. Exclude _____
   b. General concept: _____
   _____

4. harmony
   peace
   prosperous
   moribund

   a. Exclude _____
   b. General concept: _____
   _____

5. stark
   plain
   specter
   undecorated

   a. Exclude _____
   b. General concept: _____
   _____

A.5 DIRECTIONS: For each of the following items, give an example that demonstrates your understanding of the boldfaced word.

6. A *blight* that might hit college campuses _____

_____

7. Two things an *angler* needs _____

_____

8. Something, other than a bee, that *drones* _____

_____

9. Two countries that live in *harmony* _____

_____

10. A situation in which your home or your dorm room might look *stark* ____

_____

READING B

Reading B, "The Education of Berenice Belizaire," by Joe Klein, tells the story of a young Haitian immigrant who arrived in New York unable to speak English, was treated meanly by her classmates, yet became valedictorian of her high school class. This selection also tells a larger story—the story of how immigrants influence education in this country and how education influences immigrants. Before reading this selection, think for a moment about your own schooling. Did your high school have a large number of immigrants in its student body? Did immigrant students tend to be hardworking? What issues do immigrant students have to deal with that nonimmigrant students do not have to face? Before reading the article and completing the Vocabulary Activities, evaluate your present understanding of each of the 14 targeted words. Circle 1, 2, or 3 to indicate how familiar you are with each word (see page 4 for an explanation of the rating system).

Level of Understanding

corroded	1	2	3
elite	1	2	3
enduring	1	2	3
inebriated	1	2	3
median	1	2	3
menial	1	2	3
perverse	1	2	3
preconceived	1	2	3

prodding	1	2	3
propriety	1	2	3
reinvigorated	1	2	3
spurn	1	2	3
·taunts (noun)	1	2	3
valedictory	1	2	3

The Education of Berenice Belizaire   *by Joe Klein*

When Berenice Belizaire arrived in New York from Haiti with her mother and sister in 1987, she was not very happy. She spoke no English. The family had to live in a cramped Brooklyn apartment, a far cry from the comfortable house they'd had in Haiti. Her mother, a nurse, worked long hours. School was torture. Berenice had always been a good student, but now she was learning a new language while **enduring** constant **taunts** from the Americans (both black and white). They cursed her in the cafeteria and threw food at her. Someone hit her sister in the head with a book. "Why can't we go home?" Berenice asked her mother.

Because home was too dangerous. The schools weren't always open anymore, and education—her mother insisted—was the most important thing. Her mother had always pushed her: memorize everything, she ordered. "I have a pretty good memory," Berenice admitted last week. Indeed, the other kids at school began to notice that Berenice always, somehow, knew the answers. "They started coming to me for help," she says. "They never called me a nerd."

Within two years Berenice was speaking English, though not well enough to get into one of New York's **elite** public high schools. She had to settle for the neighborhood school, James Madison—which is one of the magical American places, the alma mater of Ruth Bader Ginsburg among others, a school with a history of unlikely success stories. "I didn't realize what we had in Berenice at first," says math teacher Judith Khan. "She was good at math, but she was quiet. And the things she didn't know! She applied for a summer program in Buffalo and asked me how to get there on the subway. But she always seemed to ask the right questions. She understood the big ideas. She could think on her feet. She could explain difficult problems so the other kids could understand them. Eventually, I realized: she wasn't just pushing for grades, she was hungry for *knowl-*

edge . . . And you know, it never occurred to me that she also was doing it in English and history, all these other subjects that had to be much tougher for her than math."

She moved from third in her class to first during senior year. She was selected as valedictorian, an honor she almost refused (still shy, she wouldn't allow her picture in the school's yearbook). She gave the speech, after some **prodding**—a modest address about the importance of hard work and how it's never too late to try hard: an immigrant's **valedictory**. Last week I caught up with Berenice at the Massachusetts Institute of Technology where she was jump-starting her college career. I asked her what she wanted to be doing in 10 years: "I want to build a famous computer, like IBM," she said. "I want my name to be part of it."

Berenice Belizaire's story is remarkable, but not unusual. The New York City schools are bulging with overachieving immigrants. The burdens they place on a creaky, **corroded** system are often cited as an argument against liberal immigration policies, but teachers like Judith Khan don't seem to mind. "They're why I love teaching in Brooklyn," she says. "They have a drive in them we no longer seem to have. You see these kids, who aren't prepared academically and can barely speak the language, struggling so hard. They just sop it up. They're like little sponges. You see Berenice, who had none of the usual, **preconceived** racial barriers in her mind—you see her becoming friendly with the Russian kids, and learning chess from Po Ching [from Taiwan]. It is *so* exciting."

Dreamy hothouse: Indeed, it is possible that immigrant energy **reinvigorated** not just some schools (and more than a few teachers)—but *the city itself* in the 1980s. "Without them, New York would have been a smaller place, a poorer place, a lot less vital and exciting," says Prof. Emanuel Tobier of New York University. They restored the retail life of the city, starting a raft of small businesses—and doing the sorts of entry-level, bedpan-emptying jobs that nonimmigrants **spurn**. They added far more to the local economy than they removed; more important, they reminded enlightened New Yorkers that the city had always worked best as a vast, noisy, dreamy hothouse for the cultivation of new Americans.

The Haitians have followed the classic pattern. They have a significantly higher work-force participation rate than the average in New York. They have a lower rate of poverty. They have a higher rate of new-business formation and a lower rate of welfare dependency. Their **median** household income, at $28,853, is about $1,000 less than the citywide median (but almost $1,000 higher than Chinese immigrants, often seen as a "model" minority). They've also developed a traditional network of fraternal societies, newspapers and neighborhoods with solid—extended, rather than nuclear—families. "A big issue now is whether women who graduate from school should be allowed to live by themselves before they marry," says Lola Poisson, who counsels Haitian immigrants. "There's a lot of tension over that."

Such **perverse propriety** cannot last long. Immigrants become Americans very quickly. Some lose hope after years of **menial** labor; others lose discipline, **inebriated** by freedom. "There's an interesting phenomenon," says Philip Kasinitz of Williams College. "When immigrant kids criticize each other for getting lazy or loose, they say, 'You're becoming American.'" (Belizaire said she and the Russians would tease each other that way at Madison.) It's ironic, Kasinitz adds. "Those who work hardest to keep American culture at bay have the best chance of becoming American success stories." If so, we may be fixed on the wrong issue. The question shouldn't be whether immigrants are ruining America, but whether America is ruining the immigrants. ■

Comprehension Quick-Check

After reading "The Education of Berenice Belizaire," ask your instructor for a copy of the Comprehension Quick-Check Quiz.

Building Blocks Revisited

As you will note in the first Figuring It Out activity, several of the words in Reading B contain word elements. As discussed in Chapter 4, word elements can be useful in determining or recalling the meaning of words. See if you can pick out the targeted words that have prefixes. Do you recall what each prefix means?

Another strategy that might be helpful in this chapter is the keyword strategy, coupled with imagery. For instance, if you are having difficulty remembering the meaning of the word **prodding**, you might try using this keyword strategy:

The word **prodding** means "encouraging" or "stimulating." In the word **prodding** is the smaller word **rod**. Using the word **rod** as a stimulus for an image, picture yourself holding a fishing **rod** in your hand. You are fishing in a quiet lake for perch, a large northern fish. Use the **p** in **perch** to remember the **p** that precedes **rod**.

Your keyword sentence could be this: I do not have to prod myself into spending a quiet day with my fishing **rod** at a lake filled with **perch**. Your image might look something like the following:

Put this image and keyword sentence on your vocabulary card. You could make a similar keyword sentence and image with the words *spurn* (use the little word *urn*) and *taunt* (use the little word *aunt*).

Of course, making vocabulary cards is a good strategy to use with almost any word. As you are looking these words up in the dictionary, don't forget what you learned in Chapter 3 about effective dictionary definitions.

Vocabulary Activities

 ### Figuring It Out

B.1 DIRECTIONS: Two of the 14 targeted words from Reading B have prefixes. Using your knowledge of prefixes, answer the following questions.

1. Which word begins with a prefix meaning "to repeat or do over again"?

_____

2. What other words do you know that begin with that prefix? Check a dictionary for two examples of words that are new to you. Write each below and then provide a definition for each.

   a. _____

   b. _____

3. Which word begins with a prefix meaning "before"?

   _____

4. The word you wrote for item 3 can be altered in form to become a noun. Using your dictionary or your knowledge of suffixes, write that noun form on the line below.

   _____

5. Check your dictionary to determine whether the word *propriety* contains the prefix *pro-*. You will find that information in the etymological entry. Does the word *propriety* contain the prefix *pro-*? Yes or no? _____ If it does not, what are the root and origin of the word *propriety*?

   _____

B.2 DIRECTIONS: Answer the following questions about the 14 targeted words from Reading B.

6. Which noun means "the middle value in a series of numbers"?

   _____

7. What plural noun means "insulting remarks or statements"?

   _____

8. What verb means "to reject or refuse in a hateful manner"?

   _____

9. What adjective means "lowly in reputation"?

   _____

10. What adjective means "the best or most skilled of a group of people"?

    _____

11. What noun means "encouragement to take action"?

    _____

12. What noun means "a farewell speech or address"?

    _____

13. What adjective means "to be drunk or to be overwhelmed with excitement"?

    _____

14. What adjective means "suffering or lasting through some event or action for a long period of time"?

    _____

15. What adjective means "opposing what is typically accepted"?

    _____

16. What adjective means "decided on in advance"?

    _____

17. What adjective means "worn away or gradually dissolved over time"?

    _____

18. What noun means "proper behavior"?

    _____

19. What verb means "again gave energy and life to something or someone"?

    _____

Practicing It

B.3 DIRECTIONS: Answer the following questions, making sure to provide enough detail to demonstrate your understanding of the bold-faced words.

1. Describe some tasks that most college students consider to be *menial*.

   _____

2. What is the *median* of the following numbers: 12, 14, 15, 16, 17?

   _____

3. Would most people *spurn* an inheritance of one million dollars? Why or why not?

   _____

4. Would an individual described as *elite* have to endure hunger or homelessness? Why or why not?

   _____

5. Describe one technique for *reinvigoration* that you have used after reading and studying for a long period of time.

   _____

6. Give an example of a *taunt* that a young child might say on the playground.

   _____

7. What might a college senior say in her *valedictory* address?

   _____

8. What two factors tend to *corrode* a classroom environment?

   _____

9. Give an example of a *preconceived* opinion that many college students hold. How do you know this?

_____

10. Would a student who has to be *prodded* in the morning to get out of bed choose to take an eight o'clock class? Why or why not?

_____

11. Would someone who routinely behaves at work in a *perverse* manner be a candidate for promotion? Why or why not?

_____

12. On what occasions do individuals become *inebriated* with joy? Give two examples.

_____

13. *Propriety* is valued in many situations. Describe two instances in which you were careful to act with *propriety*.

_____

14. Does a student show determination if she *endures* the semester even though her mother is very ill? Why or why not?

_____

Applying It

B.4 DIRECTIONS: Complete the following sentences, being as specific as possible in order to demonstrate your understanding of the bold-faced word.

1. In her *valedictory* address she encouraged her classmates to _____

_____ .

2. The students became *reinvigorated* when they _____

_____ .

3. After constant *prodding* from his parents, Carlos _____

_____ .

4. The *median* grade on the first exam _____

_____ .

5. When people have *preconceived* ideas about _____

_____ .

6. The college senior *spurned* the job offer from IBM because _____

_____ .

7. After receiving *taunts* about her clothes, Marissa _____

_____ .

8. The new employee was assigned *menial* tasks such as _____

_____ .

9. The secretary's *perverse* attitude at work caused _____

_____ .

10. *Elite* colleges and universities can expect students to _____

_____ .

11. After *enduring* years of sacrifice, the struggling student _____

_____ .

12. Occasions in which *propriety* and respectfulness are expected include

_____

_____ .

13. Time and pollution *corroded* the bridge so that _____

_____ .

14. Senator Hendricks became so *inebriated* with power that he _____

_____ .

READING C

When you hear the phrase "rich and successful," you probably think of people like Donald Trump or Bill Gates because they are so frequently discussed in the media. There are, however, some very rich and successful people whom we never read about in the newspapers because they live and go about their business in a quiet and modest manner. Steve Case, the creator of AOL (America Online), is such an individual. As you read this article, ask yourself this question: What characteristics made Steve Case so successful? Before reading the article and completing the Vocabulary Activities, evaluate your present understanding of each of the 23 targeted words. Circle 1, 2, or 3 to indicate how familiar you are with each word (see page 4 for an explanation of the rating system).

	Level of Understanding		
adversity	1	2	3
affirmation	1	2	3
banal	1	2	3
eerie	1	2	3
empathetic	1	2	3
entrepreneur	1	2	3
flamboyant	1	2	3
flaunt	1	2	3
fledgling	1	2	3
glitches	1	2	3
imperturbable	1	2	3
introverted	1	2	3
mockery	1	2	3

nascent	1	2	3
philanthropist	1	2	3
racked	1	2	3
relentlessly	1	2	3
schmoozing	1	2	3
succinctly	1	2	3
synergy	1	2	3
unostentatious	1	2	3
unpretentious	1	2	3
venture (adjective)	1	2	3

The Players: Case Study

by Jared Sandberg, with Elizabeth Angell and Jennifer Tanaka

The rich, famous and powerful are, typically, bundles of insecurity. Winning politicians like Bill Clinton need constant doses of love and **affirmation.** Tycoons like Donald Trump often **flaunt** their fortunes with expensive toys and trophy wives. Even geeky techno-zillionaires like Bill Gates indulge in cults of personality. Steve Case, who last week became about as rich and famous as a businessman can be, doesn't appear to require the usual trappings or badges of success. He lives in a nonflashy house in a quiet Virginia suburb (no pool or tennis court) and drives comfortable but **unostentatious** cars (an SUV and a VW bug). His corporate offices afford a clear view of some power lines and easy access to Wal-Mart. Neither warm nor **empathetic,** he is regarded by many observers as something of a bore, **relentlessly** on message, impersonal in manner. His dress is dull: he is a walking commercial for khaki pants (he once posed for a Gap ad). He likes colorful Hawaiian shirts, but on Case, they somehow look like drab oxford cloth.

He is driven, but not by some inner hurt or buried longing. He has not been forged by **adversity;** he does not so much face down the naysayers as shrug them off. His modest and low-key father, a corporate lawyer in Honolulu, takes no credit for his son's success. "It wasn't us," he told *Newsweek.* "We merely supported him." Case has no overarching philosophy, save a **banal** mantra: "To change people's lives."

From "The Players: Case Study," by Jared Sanberg, with Elizabeth Angell and Jennifer Tanaka, *Newsweek,* January 24, 2000, © 2000, Newsweek, Inc. All rights reserved. Reprinted by permission.

What Case, 41, has in abundance is self-confidence. He doesn't show off because he doesn't need to. He appears to always know where he wants to go, and how to get there. He was able to see, before others, a global medium that would change the way people live, learn and work. He did not discover the promise of the interconnected world by trial and error or a painful process of self-discovery. He seems guided by a gyroscope, an internal compass. His story is a lesson in what a very smart man with a simple vision can do—if he isn't thrown off by fads and **mockery** and the usual demands of vanity and ego.

Case's early experiments and hobbies foreshadow his later accomplishments in almost **eerie** detail. His family is part of the old white Anglo establishment of Honolulu. He grew up sure of his place in an upscale but **unpretentious** neighborhood, near an exclusive private school he attended where the students were allowed to go barefoot. He was raised to believe that "self-worth does not get measured by toys," said his brother, Dan, a multimillionaire who drives an eight-year-old car. "Our parents didn't teach it; they modeled it." Dan was the outgoing one, the crowd pleaser who went on from Princeton to become a Rhodes scholar and a rich **venture** capitalist. Steve was quieter, more inner-directed. He was also the **entrepreneur.** As boys, Dan and Steve started their own company, Case Enterprises (they referred to their rooms as "offices"). Steve recalled their brotherly **synergy:** "I'd come up with the idea," said Steve, who would sometimes awaken his brother in the middle of the night with an inspiration.

Case Enterprises' main "business" was essentially a marketing scheme based on a paper route. Steve used his access to the neighbors' homes to peddle everything from seeds to watches to personalized Christmas cards. Learning to type in the seventh grade, Steve sent away for anything he could get free, thus getting himself on mailing lists for records, consumer-product samples and other geegaws. His family recalled that he was eager to be first to the mailbox every day. (Steve, you've got mail!)

At Williams College in Massachusetts, Case kept on marketing: limos from the campus to the airport, fruit baskets, rock-concert tickets. Case wasn't **flamboyant,** although he sang in a rock band a few times before small audiences. In the library he studied trade publications like *Advertising Age*—and saw, clearly for the first time, the future.

While his classmates pondered Shakespeare and played beer pong, Case began reading about the **nascent** cable-TV business. To learn more, he got a job selling cable door to door one summer in Hawaii. In his cover letters for a full-time job after college, he stated his vision **succinctly:** "Innovations in telecommunications (especially two-way cable systems) will result in our television sets (big screen, of course!) becoming an information line, newspaper, school, computer, referendum machines, and catalog." One application went to Time Inc.'s new cable entertainment company, HBO. The boss of HBO at the time was Gerald Levin. Case was rejected for the job. The year was 1980.

His first jobs taught him how to get close to the consumer, and that technology is a means, not an end. The biggest lesson he learned was to keep things simple and predictable. He bought his first computer in 1982, a clunky Kaypro, which he thought was too difficult to use (Case had done poorly in a computer class at Williams). No matter: through his modem, he discovered the then sparsely traveled online world.

Here was the gateway to market to the masses. Through his brother's venture-capital connections, he entered the *fledgling* online business in the early '80s, surviving various shakeouts until, by 1991, he was president of America Online. His path was precarious but revealing. Case was forever sneered at by the digerati of Silicon Valley for being too low tech, even a little cheesy. But Case didn't care about being cool. He wasn't interested in the latest technological wrinkle. He wanted his system to be simple, so that anyone could use it. While his bigger and seemingly more powerful competitors like CompuServe, owned by H&R Block, and Prodigy, backed by Sears and IBM, fell by the wayside, AOL plunged ahead. Case discovered that his customers were most interested in chatting—usually about sex, it turns out—but in any case they cared more about easy access to each other than mastering the latest techie tricks.

Case understood his own limitations, as well as the wants of his customers. Jim Kimsey, an early mentor and former chairman of AOL, recalled that when AOL went public in 1992, Case was warned by the investment bankers that he lacked the *schmoozing* skills to be a good front man. Swallowing his ego, Case stepped aside as CEO and gave the job to Kimsey. Case is regarded as a bit of a stiff by reporters and other industry executives. (Case can be "as cold as Spock on a bad day," said one business rival.) By his employees, however, he is seen as *imperturbable* and intensely loyal. Turnover among top managers at AOL has been comparatively low.

Case's team needed to have faith in the mid-'90s, when the company was *racked* by crises and experts routinely wrote it off. Overextended in its effort to reach the masses, the company suffered technical *glitches* and charges that it was using sleazy marketing practices. Prosecutors in 39 states threatened to sue AOL for questionable billing methods. Responding to intense price competition from cheaper Internet services, the company replaced its hourly fees with a flat-rate pricing scheme. But executives underestimated demand, and overeager surfers couldn't log on, enraging consumers.

AOL survived in part because Case was able to convey his quiet confidence to jittery customers, and because he was able to move more quickly and decisively to fix problems than his corporate competitors.

Case does not forget that bicoastal elitists predicted the demise of AOL. He can remind reporters of their wrongheaded predictions from long ago. But he does so without rancor. These days he has loosened up a bit. He is becoming a big-time *philanthropist,* already giving away nearly $200 million of his fortune (an estimated $1.4 billion). He has become a statesman of the Wired World, explaining the interconnected future to the lawmakers who will regulate it. When need be, he can pose. Last week he clowned for photographers in the AOL company store, draping a good-humored Gerald Levin with AOL sweatshirts, hats and Windbreakers, laughingly recalling HBO had once turned him down for a job. Earlier, in an interview with Newsweek, he indulged in rare introspection. "I'm probably not as *introverted* as people think," he said. "And I don't resent the attention as much as people think." Case keeps a "zone of privacy," he said. "I like the fact that I might go to the White House or be on the 'Today' show but then go with my kids to a movie at a shopping center and for the most part be unrecognized. The ability to have a normal life is actually what I'm trying to preserve." Trying to shuttle him between interviews and public appearances, his office tried to arrange a car and driver for him last week. No thanks, said Case. He preferred to drive himself. ■

Comprehension Quick-Check

After reading "The Players: Case Study," ask your instructor for a copy of the Comprehension Quick-Check Quiz.

Building Blocks Revisited

You can use a variety of generative vocabulary strategies to help you master the 23 targeted words in Reading C at a conceptual level. If you decide to make vocabulary cards, an effective strategy for such a lengthy list of words, you might want to group your cards into categories. For example, you could group the words according to whether they have positive or negative connotations (*banal, relentlessly,* and *flamboyant* share some negative connotations).

As you use the dictionary to locate definitions, consider the following three points. First and most important, you will need to use both context and the dictionary in a careful and insightful manner in order to develop correct definitions. For example, the dictionary provides only a beginning point for *affirmation* and *synergy.* You will need to supplement the definitions with information from the article. Second, you should select the correct definition that fits the meaning and the way the word is used in the sentence. The word *rack,* for example, has at least eight different entries. As you read the dictionary entries, also note that two of the targeted words—*schmoozing* and *glitches*—originate from Yiddish and that one word—*philanthropist*—has an interesting Greek and Latin origin. Third, it may seem at first glance that your dictionary does not contain some of the words: ***unostentatious, relentlessly,*** and ***unpretentious.*** However, if you remove the prefixes or suffixes from these words, you will be able to find them in your dictionary.

Vocabulary Activities

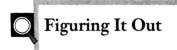

Figuring It Out

C.1 DIRECTIONS: Fill in each blank with the appropriate targeted word from Reading C.

Targeted Word	*Definition*
1. _____	modest, not showy
2. _____	young, inexperienced
3. _____	bad luck, hardship, misfortune
4. _____	lacking freshness and originality
5. _____	ridicule, scorn, an insulting imitation
6. _____	emerging, just coming into existence
7. _____	collective effort that creates an effect greater than the sum of the individual contributions
8. _____	weird, mysterious, almost supernatural
9. _____	dangerous, daring, risky, hazardous
10. _____	minor mishaps or problems
11. _____	strained, tormented
12. _____	unshakably calm, cool, and collected
13. _____	able to identify with other people's feelings
14. _____	without yielding or showing pity, persistently

Targeted Word	*Definition*
15. _____	someone who organizes, operates, and assumes the risks and profits of a business
16. _____	plain, not trying to show off or impress others
17. _____	in a few words, tersely
18. _____	highly elaborate, ornate, flashy
19. _____	chatting with other people in an easy manner
20. _____	statement declaring someone or something to be valuable, true, or good
21. _____	focused inward rather than on the external environment
22. _____	someone who cares about others and gives money and time to charities
23. _____	to show off, to parade about in a flashy manner

Practicing It

C.2 DIRECTIONS: Read each sentence carefully. If the boldfaced word is used correctly, circle *C* and go on to the next item. If the boldfaced word is used incorrectly, circle *I* and then make the sentence correct.

C   I   **1.** Because his life was filled with so much ***adversity,*** the student was always happy.

C   I   **2.** Most politicians are known for their ***succinct*** way of speaking on important issues.

C   I   **3.** After riding his bicycle for 120 miles, the cyclist was ***racked*** by pain and fatigue.

C   I   **4.** The ***fledgling*** author knew exactly how to write and publish a best-selling novel.

C   I   **5.** ***Banal*** jokes are the ones that make most people laugh.

C I   **6.** Dedicated athletes often put themselves through *relentless* practices and drills in order to make sure they will win.

C I   **7.** Because the millionaire was also a *philanthropist,* he decided to spend all his money on personal pleasures such as cars, boats, and houses across the world.

C I   **8.** Most celebrities are known for their *unpretentious* clothing and hairstyles.

C I   **9.** At the Academy Award and Grammy Award shows performers receive *affirmation* of their acting or singing abilities.

C I **10.** Most people are worried that their computer programs will crash because of *glitches*.

C I **11.** Because the child was afraid of the dark and disliked *eerie* happenings, he always looked forward to Halloween.

C I **12.** The used-car salesperson was very skilled at *schmoozing* with customers.

C I **13.** The *introverted* college freshman was thrilled when his professor assigned him to deliver a speech to the large lecture class.

C I **14.** Five years ago, using the Internet to make a hotel or airplane reservation involved learning a *nascent* technology for most individuals.

C I **15.** After enduring considerable *mockery* from the audience during his speech, the politician thanked his listeners for their kind words of encouragement and appreciation.

C I **16.** Effective nurses usually display some *empathy* for the pain their patients feel.

C I **17.** Most rock stars reject *flamboyant* openings to their concerts because they are *unostentatious* individuals.

C I **18.** When we are seriously ill and need surgery, we typically want an *imperturbable* doctor who makes wise decisions.

C I **19.** Because she was a successful *entrepreneur,* she preferred not to take any risks with the new business located in the shopping mall.

C I **20.** The *synergy* between the owner and chef of the restaurant helped to make the place world famous for its decor and visually appealing food.

C I **21.** The basketball player decided to *flaunt* his athletic talents by slam-dunking the ball several times during the game.

C I **22.** Many of the young *venture* capitalists prefer not to invest in technology because of the risks.

 Applying It

C . 3 DIRECTIONS: Complete the following analogies using the targeted words listed below.

imperturbable   fledgling
philanthropist   relentless
synergy   unostentatious
racked

1. flamboyant : _____ :: creative : banal

2. experienced : _____ :: normal : eerie

3. giving up : _____ :: wordy and vague : succinct

4. established : nascent :: _____ : nervous

5. venture : entrepreneur :: empathetic : _____

C . 4 DIRECTIONS: Answer the following questions, making sure to provide enough detail to demonstrate your understanding of the boldfaced words.

6. Would an *unpretentious* billionaire *flaunt* his wealth? Why or why not?

_____

_____

7. Would an individual *racked* with insecurity and low self-esteem need *affirmation* from other individuals? Why or why not?

_____

_____

8. Would an **introverted** individual be comfortable in a job that required her to **schmooze** with potential clients and customers? Why or why not?

_____

_____

9. Would most people consider it an **adversity** if their new VCR had several **glitches** in its programming capabilities? Why or why not?

_____

_____

10. Would it be important for two **entrepreneurs** working together on a creative and important project to experience **synergy**? Why or why not?

_____

_____

11. Would it be a wise idea for a **fledgling** employee to **mock** the way his supervisor conducts the weekly meetings? Why or why not?

_____

_____

 ## Extending

C.5 DIRECTIONS: There are 49 targeted words in Chapter 7. As you review them and your strategies, think about the words with a positive connotation and those with a negative connotation. Listed below are 9 of the 49 words. List the words that have a positive connotation in the left column and the words that have a negative connotation in the right column. Then add 6 more words—2 from each reading in Chapter 7. Omit words that have neither a positive nor a negative connotation. Be ready to justify your selections in groups or with a classmate.

menial	moribund	inebriated
valedictory	empathetic	banal
pretentious	perverse	reinvigorated

Positive	*Negative*
_____	_____
_____	_____
_____	_____
_____	_____
_____	_____
_____	_____
_____	_____
_____	_____
_____	_____
_____	_____
_____	_____
_____	_____

Evaluating

Review and test yourself on the 49 targeted words in Chapter 7. Then ask your instructor for the comprehensive exam on these words.

INDEX